HOME FRONT YORKSHIRE

EAST RIDING OF YORKSHIRE L.I.S.	
901225701	
Bertrams	20.06.08
940.534281	£19.99
COT.	L.S.

HOME FRONT YORKSHIRE 1939–1945

'What did you do in the war granddad?'

Len Markham

“Old Fireworks is are hedmaster an he ses that scuwl must shut cos of a bully called Mister Hickler. I dont care how big the bugga is. If he tuchis my rabbits arl bray im.”
(Lucy Higginbottom's Diary)

Pen & Sword
MILITARY

First published in Great Britain in 2007 by
PEN & SWORD MILITARY
an imprint of
Pen & Sword Books Ltd
47 Church Street
Barnsley
South Yorkshire
S70 2AS

Copyright © Len Markham, 2007

ISBN 978-1-84415-628-3

The right of Len Markham to be identified as author of this work
has been asserted by him in accordance with the
Copyright, Designs and Patents Act 1988.

A CIP catalogue record for this book is
available from the British Library.

All rights reserved. No part of this book may be reproduced or
transmitted in any form or by any means, electronic or mechanical
including photocopying, recording or by any information storage and
retrieval system, without permission from the publisher in writing.

Typeset by Concept, Huddersfield, West Yorkshire
Printed and bound in Great Britain by CPI UK

Pen & Sword Books Ltd incorporates the imprints of
Pen & Sword Aviation, Pen & Sword Maritime, Pen & Sword Military,
Wharncliffe Local History, Pen & Sword Select,
Pen & Sword Military Classics and Leo Cooper.

For a complete list of Pen & Sword titles please contact
PEN & SWORD BOOKS LIMITED
47 Church Street, Barnsley, South Yorkshire, S70 2AS, England.
E-mail: enquiries@pen-and-sword.co.uk
Website: www.pen-and-sword.co.uk

Contents

This book is dedicated to the wonderful memory of ace rabbit catcher and stockman Dennis Simpson (1926–2006) who throughout a most productive life continued to bring home the bacon.

Introduction

It was the most memorable radio broadcast in British history:

"This morning the British Ambassador in Berlin handed the German government a final note stating that unless we heard from them by eleven o'clock that they were prepared at once to withdraw their troops from Poland a state of war would exist between us. I have to tell you now that no such undertaking has been received, and that consequently this country is at war with Germany."

The doleful monotone announcement by Prime Minister Neville Chamberlain from the Cabinet Room at No. 10 Downing Street at 11.15 on the morning of Sunday 3 September 1939 left the nation stunned and wondering.

Over the proceeding few years, there had been an inexorable slide to war. Adolf Hitler came to power in Germany in 1933, his Nationalsozialistische Deutsche Arbeiterpartei (NAZI Party) promising to revitalise Germany, to reverse the humiliations suffered as a consequence of the Treaty of Versailles, to halt economic decline and to purge the nation of Jews, Communists and other undesirables. The downtrodden German consciousness was awoken. Pride and self-belief were restored and the new charismatic Reichskanzler soon held a stranglehold on the national destiny.

In direct treaty violation in 1935, he reintroduced conscription and set about rebuilding the army, navy and air force. In 1936 his troops reoccupied the demilitarised zone in the Rhineland and the newly equipped Luftwaffe sent troops to help Franco in the Spanish Civil War, tactic and equipment proving air raids by Stuka dive bombers on such undefended targets as the civilian town of Guernica causing international outrage. But even this atrocity, coupled with the Austrian *Anchluss* and the invasion of the Czechoslovakian Sudetenland in 1938 failed to alert the world to the NAZI menace. It seems hard to credit now, but at the very time that the Panzer divisions were being mobilised to carve up the continent, the well respected international magazine *TIME* announced their Man of the Year for 1938. It was none other than a lionised Adolf Hitler. Give a bully an inch and he will surely take your back yard.

The mood in the United Kingdom was reflective and sombre. Flowers on the graves of the soldiers who perished in the 'war to end all wars' were still being tended and the financial costs of the millions of tons of bombs and shells used in the conflict were still being calculated as the population mulled on the prophetic words of Chamberlain's predecessor, Stanley Baldwin. In 1935 he predicted: 'There is one thing which differentiates modern war . . . and that is the increase in the horror of war, and the tacit assumption on the part of all nations, that the civil community will no longer be immune from the horrors of warfare as they have been since the barbarous ages.' Baldwin's stark predictions were reinforced by Pathe newsreels in cinemas, stark footage of the atrocities perpetrated by German and Italian bombers on defenceless civilian populations in Spain and Abyssinia, coupled with an alarming forecast of 66,000 British dead and 134,000 injured in the very first week of hostilities causing widespread fear. The prior distribution of thirty-eight million gas masks to civilians in 1938 and the publication in July 1939 of a government leaflet – *Some Things You Should Know If War Should Come* (issued to every home in the country) – had forewarned the civilian population of the impending horrors like no previous warnings in history.

Suddenly, every facet of normal life was subservient to the war effort and to just staying alive. By the end of 1931, unemployment in Britain had reached 3 million but the spectre of depression and the clamours of the Jarrow marchers had been dissipated by the drive to mass rearmament to counter the Nazi threat. Now though, vast sections of the workforce were appropriated to the military, conscription, brought in initially in May 1939 under the Military Training Act, requiring all men between twenty and twenty-one years of age to undergo six months' training. On the day war was declared, the National Services (Armed Forces) Act made all eighteen to forty-one year old men liable for conscription, although men in 'reserved occupations' vital to the war effort were exempt.

As men went off to fight, week-by-week, regulations were tightened governing every aspect of civilian life. Ration books were issued in October 1939 and food rationing began at the beginning of January 1940. Clothes rationing followed in June 1941. Mail was censored, blackout restrictions were imposed, weather forecasting was curtailed to deny vital information to the enemy, property was requisitioned for military purposes, travel movements were restricted, wireless programmes were reorganised and families traumatised by the conscription of fathers and sons were further dismembered by the voluntary evacuation of children from vulnerable production centres like Hull, Sheffield and Middlesbrough.

As the situation worsened and the new Prime Minister, Winston Churchill defined the 'blood, sweat and tears' struggle ahead, those left at home found themselves urged to even greater efforts, women taking on heavy manual work in factories, fields and on the railway network, old men becoming air raid wardens and members of the Home Guard and children, between lessons, collecting hedgerow fruits for jam making, and acting as messengers and fire watching. Galvanised by the distinct possibility of annihilation and invasion, the entire British nation was regulated and mobilised like never before but it responded, for the most part, in tireless unison, the Herculean efforts of the majority of the civilian population keeping the guns firing to victory.

Morale and motivation were everything. Any hint of negativity was suppressed and in the battle for hearts and minds, jingoistic propaganda was the key, the almost daily issuing and promulgation of posters, leaflets and infinitely proscriptive rules and regulations seeking to marshal and control a unified march against Nazism. But not everyone was in step.

In any conflict, there will always be opportunistic individuals who will exploit problems for self-gain, the multiple adversities of the Second World War providing chances aplenty. During blackout conditions, heartless burglars moved with heightened boldness and anonymity and less chance of detection. Looters preyed on bombed out and empty houses and commercial premises. Black marketeers operated on foggy street corners and furtively in pubs and clubs, capitalising on critical shortages of consumer goods and cutting shady deals with unscrupulous officials. Confidence tricksters took advantage of mounting fears and phobias selling dubious concoctions and wares and the shortage of building materials coupled with the insatiable demand for constructional goods lead to massive contract and tender fraud. Turn your back on a building site for a moment ... and it was gone! Even tarpaulins, hurriedly draped over bomb craters, were snatched in the blink of an eye.

It has to be said though that 'everybody was at it', hunger, cold and the craving for excessively rationed and luxury goods making minor criminals of almost the entire population. Hoarding of more than a week's supply of food and provisions was outlawed and it became illegal to trade ration coupons, several high profile arrests serving to highlight the extent of the problems. The actor and playwright Noel Coward was twice fined for currency infringements. Popular dance bandleader Victor Silvester was fined for smuggling offences and the actor/songwriter Ivor Novello who paradoxically wrote the fervently nationalistic hit song *Keep the Home Fires Burning*, was sent to prison for eight weeks for fraudulently obtaining petrol coupons for his Rolls Royce car.

The penalties for stepping out of line were indeed severe, draconian legal measures and newly conferred powers on officialdom encouraging every petty tyrant to strut from obscurity to harass, coerce and report transgressors, often for comparatively minor offences. Blackout regulations were enforced with excessive zeal. On one occasion police were summoned to a house besieged by a braying mob. They were attempting to smash down the door of an elderly man, their ferocity provoked by unscreened lights from two front rooms. The man, aged eighty-three, was arrested, taken to court and fined £2 – the equivalent of four times the weekly pension rate for a single person. Alerted to a similar blackout violation, police attended another address and, finding the door locked, shot out the offending bulbs with a rifle! In one bizarre case, the Witchcraft Act of 1735 was invoked to prosecute a celebrity medium. She paid for her crime of allegedly reuniting a retired Indian Army Captain with his son who was reported missing in action in May 1940, with nine months in gaol. One man was taken into custody for photographing an electricity pylon and dozens of people were brought before the courts for smoking during air raids on the premise that the red-hot cigarette ends would enable Luftwaffe pilots to find their targets. And it got much worse. You could be bundled into a Black Maria for throwing rice or confetti at a wedding. Housewives could be hauled in for putting out washing at night, queue jumping might lead to a night in the cells, sleeping in an un-camouflaged tent risked confiscation and censure and the release of a racing pigeon without prior written permission from a police officer could lead to an arrest for spying. And of course, it became a criminal offence to bake or sell white loaves. We missed a totalitarian state by a whisker.

Assaulted by such a plethora of rules and regulations and assailed on all sides by armies of enforcing 'Little Hitlers' most civilian populations would have pulled out their collective hairs and become paranoid. Not so the phlegmatic British, the practical people of England's biggest county particularly responding to the six year challenge with typical pluck and determination.

The county was a major centre for industrial production, the cities of Sheffield, Leeds and Hull and dozens of smaller towns manufacturing vital ordnance, equipment, components, chemicals and clothing for the war effort, thousands of miners in the Yorkshire coalfield keeping the pistons pumping in their production of vital fuel. Lister's giant mill in Manningham made parachute material, the English Steel Corporation in Sheffield, for a time, had the only steam-powered press capable of producing Rolls Royce Merlin crankshafts for fighter aircraft. A sister factory, David Brown's in Meltham, again for limited period, was the sole manufacturer of Spitfire gears. And in a highly secretive operation, the chemical specialist ICI stepped up production of mustard gas supplies in Huddersfield on the direct orders of insistent Prime Minister, Winston Churchill. On a smaller scale, Swifts in Scarborough specialised in the supply of ammunition boxes, oil drums and air raid equipment, and in Bradford, Bradford Textile clandestinely worked on Government contracts making replica German uniforms and insignia for use by resistance groups and allied agents operating in Germany and occupied Europe. Under a similar cloak of secrecy, another Bradford firm – Fields Printers – produced detailed maps for RAF navigators involved in the D-Day campaign, Leeds board game and playing card manufacturers Waddington's surreptitiously hiding maps of occupied territories in their products to assist POWs to escape.

The statistics of the period tell a tremendous tale of superhuman effort and dedication, scores of books recalling the privations, the exhaustion, the despair and the injuries and deaths brought about by accidents and the effects of enemy bombing.

"... as many people suffered just as much devastation and trauma as did the men and women in the services."

That selfless corporate story has been well told and it will not be replicated here. Rather, at the heart of this book, in Chapter 6 entitled 'Days in the Lives of ...' I would particularly like to give an airing to many previously unpublished, seemingly ordinary tales of individual people whose lives seemed humdrum and tedious at the time but whose testimonies, over sixty years on, reveal a collective dynamism that with trademark Yorkshire humour kept the home fires burning. I feel quite privileged in having had an opportunity to breath life into these memories and, in this my twenty-ninth and most personally enjoyable book to date, to acknowledge the enduring spirits and legacies of the contributors, many of whom have since passed on.

Len Markham
Eastbourne
2007

AUTHOR'S NOTE

In compiling this book, the author has been privileged to have been able to record the wartime testimonies of contributors for posterity. Such has been the overwhelming interest in this project that much valuable material has, of necessity, been temporarily put aside to feature in an ongoing second volume. If readers would like to contribute to this sequel or to an in-preparation companion volume 'FRONTLINE YORKSHIRE – What did you do in the war granddad?' could they please write to:

Len Markham
c/o Pen and Sword Books Limited
47 Church Street
Barnsley
South Yorkshire
S70 2AS

Chapter 1

Quiet Nights Out . . . and In

At the outbreak of war, in the absolute certainty that Nazi Germany posed a deadly and imminent threat from air, the government imposed immediate regulations to preserve lives. Cinemas and theatres were closed and a universal blackout was imposed, keeping millions of people at home twiddling their thumbs, ears pricked for the air raid sirens. Nothing happened and the nation slept on undisturbed but bored, author George Bernard Shaw capturing the public indignation at the closures with a stinging rebuke in *The Times*:

“May I be allowed to protest vehemently against the order to close all theatres and picture houses during the war? It seems to me to be a masterstroke of unimaginative stupidity. During the last war, we had 80,000 soldiers on leave every night. There were not enough theatres for them... we have hundreds of thousands of evacuated children to keep out of mischief and traffic dangers. Are there to be no pictures for them? The authorities should at once provide new theatres and picture houses ... all actors, variety artists' musicians and entertainers of all sorts should be exempted from every sort of service except their all-important professional one. What agent of Chancellor Hitler is it who suggested that we should all cower in darkness and terror for the duration?”

Public denunciations like Shaw's soon showed that entertainments had a vital role to play in keeping up morale and in providing a subtle outlet for propaganda, notwithstanding the dangers from air attack. 'Going to the pictures' became a weekly treat for millions of civilians, such films – black and white of course – as *Freedom Radio* (1941), *In Which We Serve* (1942), *One of our Aircraft is Missing* (1942) and *Western Approaches* (1944) helping to stiffen resolve and portray the righteousness of the stand against the Nazi's. At a time when Adolf Hitler's unmistakable face began to adorn thousands of the nation's chamber pots and dart boards, motion pictures also got in on the act, Charlie Chaplin's box office blockbuster *The Great Dictator* (1940) extracting the Adolf in a riotous lampoon by Hynkel, the Fuehrer of the XX – the Double Cross Party. Some English films had a similar comedic theme and music hall stars were recruited to offer a lively mixture of comedy and fun, George Formby starring in *Let George Do It* (1940) and the comedian Will Hay parodying German idiosyncrasies in the hilarious *The Goose Steps Out* (1942).

Hilary B. Blackburne of Hessle recalls:

“The cinema was a great escape from the harsh reality of wartime and the cinemas were always full with long queues waiting to go in for the next performance. Often, the 'Air Raid Notice' would flash onto the screen and audiences had the option of leaving or taking a risk and staying for the rest of the programme. Sometimes, going to the cinema proved to be a risky business and on one occasion several people were killed when a lone German plane dived down and machine gunned them in Hull. ”

Films provided entertainment for the masses but there were many home-grown, morale boosting events led by a phalanx of self-parodying Tykes who have a reputation of shrugging off adversity with a quip and a song, their determination to ‘keep smiling through’ producing a host of entertainments from flower shows to oddest shaped shrapnel competitions. One such contest in the West Riding mining and glass-making town of Castleford attracted national attention, the competition lifting spirits in the much bombed ‘most populated square mile’ in the British Isles.

The event dubbed ‘A Reight Neet Aht!’ was first held in 1936 as a fundraiser for a local hospital. It continued through the war years in the Cooperative Hall, attracting visiting celebrities, who participated in games such as darts, shuttlecock, skipping, battledore and the old Yorkshire favourite, marbles, better known locally as taws. Superstar George Formby, who met his wife Beryl at Castleford Theatre Royal in 1923 while she was working with her sister as part of a clog-dancing duo – *The Two Violets* – was the most famous visitor. With an affection and nostalgia for the town, George and Beryl delayed a journey to entertain troops in France in 1944 by four days to stop over in Castleford. They received a tumultuous welcome from an excited crowd, George being sworn in as the town’s ARP warden for the night to allow him to participate in the fun.

Opening the proceedings to laughter, George said: ‘It’s great to be back in Castleford because I met Beryl here when I was a little lad.’ With his usual cheeky grin and champagne jollity, he went on to flip and roll his taws in full ARP dress, hilariously hindered by a tin hat, gas mask and a variety of ridiculous false noses. The special taws for the occasion were manufactured by local glassmakers Lumb and Co and were inscribed with George’s signature; other mementoes of the evening included a presentational ash tray produced by Castleford pottery Clokies – it had a image of ‘Old Nasty’ (Hitler) in its base – and a number of signed taws for auctioning off, George scratching out his signature with the tip of a dart.

Of course, the most universal ingredient of a ‘Reight Neet Aht’ was the good old English pub, this unique and timeless institution serving as a refreshment room, meeting hall, theatre, music hall, doctor’s surgery and mini Parliament. In its taprooms and snugs, all thoughts of war were relegated for just a few fleeting hours. Its social and spiritual values were recognised by the Government and beer was not rationed although its alcoholic content was reduced to combat drunkenness and strict opening and closing times were imposed, the most dreaded phrase in the English language becoming even more forbidding during those fateful years, when the reveries of leaving the conflict behind were inexorably shattered by calls of the landlord 'Time gentlemen please!' and by the reaching out for tin hats.

Whatever the manner of the pub – street corner local, city bar or country inn – it had an abiding imagery and symbolism of Englishness that infiltrated every trench and cockpit, Charles Dickens evocations stirring the mind to relish the homecoming:

"One little roadside inn, snugly sheltered behind a great elm tree with a rare seat for idlers encircling its capacious bole, addressed a cheerful front towards the traveller. The ruddy signboard perched up in the tree with its golden letters winking in the sun, ogle eyed the passer-by, from among the green leaves, like a jolly face, and promised good cheer. The horse-trough, full of clear fresh water and the ground below it sprinkled with droppings of fragrant hay made every horse that passed prick up its ears. The crimson curtains in the lower rooms and the pure white hangings in the little bedchambers above, beckoned 'Come in!' with every breath of air. Upon the bright green shutters there were golden legends about beer and ale and neat wines and good beds; and an affecting picture of a brown jug frothing over at the top. Upon the window sills were flowering plants in bright red pots which made a lively show against the front of the house; and in the darkness of the doorway there were streaks of light which glanced off from the surface of the bottles and tankards."

The abiding reality was that pubs sometimes ran out of beer (and there is nothing worse!) but it was just such imagery that succoured Royal Canadian Air Force pilots and crew stationed at the base at RAF Linton-on-Ouse. In 1943, Linton became the home of two RCAF squadrons – 408 'Flying Goose' and 426 'Thunderbirds'. Between operations their men would gravitate to the village of Nun Monkton between Harrogate and York and the welcoming tap room of the *Alice Hawthorn* – an inn that in times past must surely have inspired Dickens to pen the above lines. The inn was just a short distance from the base but there was a problem. It was across the Ouse.

The dilemma was solved by a wily Yorkshire ferryman who, legend has it, charged 6d for the outward journey, raising his fares after closing time. Faced with either a swim or a ten mile walk along winding country lanes, the inebriated airmen nearly always paid up, although a recently published book, *The Story of Nun Monkton,* by Rosemary Enright records a piratical commandeering of the craft at closing time that resulted in fatalities. But there were more tragic deaths. In August 1943, a nine-strong sortie by 'Thunderbirds'

Squadron attacked the V1 rocket stronghold at Peenemunde inflicting severe damage. Two aircraft were lost along with their crews.

The Canadians were adopted by the villagers of Nun Monkton like long lost sons, the landlord and landlady of the *Alice Hawthorn* – Mr and Mrs Ted Dodman – making them especially welcome. Between sorties, off duty airmen ate and drank in the pub and some slept in its attic. Ted lent money to some of the men when they were short of the price of a pint and, after listening to nostalgic talk about the delights of Canadian corn-on-the-cob, the landlady promptly sent out for a packet of seeds. Within a few months, the men were tucking in. The fame of the pub grew, every successfully returning crew toasting their deliverance in Yorkshire beer and singing an anthem. Its eighth stanza went thus:

> The lads who come here again and again,
> They've no inclination to roam,
> They know very well that 'The Alice' is swell,
> They look upon it as home.

Even those who were shot down over enemy territory and incarcerated in POW camps somehow managed to get messages back to the *Alice Hawthorn*. And, although necessary security regulations cloaked the inn in anonymity, it fast became famous, a transatlantic BBC radio broadcast from its bar featuring contributions from Mr and Mrs Dodman, from villagers and from the airmen. Some time later, the Canadian statesman and diplomat Vincent Massey wrote on behalf of the Canadian nation to Ted Dodman to thank him for his hospitality. Meanwhile, back in the soporific hamlet of Nun Monkton, one Canadian flyer – he had the reputation of taking to the air in cowboy boots – upset the ducks on the pond by performing bronco stunts on the village green.

Like the waters of the ponderous Rivers Nidd and Ouse that conjoin just north of the village, details of Nun Monkton's wartime celebrity have been slow to emerge, the most obvious connections with RCAF crews being proudly displayed in a series of photographs in the largely unchanged bar of the *Alice Hawthorn* where ageing veterans have joyously been reunited from time to time. Hopeful of finding more information about its wartime role, I tapped into the internet and discovered, posted on a Canadian War Museum website, the image of a painting entitled *Airmen in a Village Pub – Yorkshire*, by well known Canadian artist Miller Brittain. He was a bomb aimer, having enlisted in the RCAF in 1942. He completed thirty-seven operational sorties in Halifax bombers and went on to win the DFC. A member of 78 Squadron which was based for a time at Linton-on-Ouse, he is depicted in his own painting, his work acknowledging the vital role of the pub 'as an antidote to the relentless, stressful and often distressing experiences of Bomber Command'. Is his depiction an interior view of the *Alice Hawthorn*? The Canadian War Museum is unsure.

Away from the pub, one famous Yorkshire haunt of aircrews even became known in the upper echelons of the Luftwaffe, *Betty's* in York regularly entertaining pilots and crews in the brief interludes between sorties. Dozens of nationalities poured through it doors to enjoy it tea parties, a hastily applied for liquor licence adding to the fun of the new *Betty's Bar*, nicknamed by allied airmen as the 'Dive' and the 'Briefing Room.' Raucous laughter, levity and humour helped mask the pre-op nerves of many flyers who never returned, the scratched signatures of some of the men – and at least one woman – who never came back surviving on a mirror in the modern cafe's basement as a poignant reminder of the war years. Some say that the habit was begun by a pilot who, in wanting to leave a personal memento behind, etched his name with a waitress's ring. *Betty's* became a national institution, an amusing cartoon in the November edition of the *Tatler* magazine showing a group of sober-looking military men tactically examining a map, one general pointing to the centre of operations with a stick, uttering the words: 'Here's Betty's Bar.'

Most people, of course, spent the majority of their leisure time at home. In millions of homes (there were 8,500,000 licence holders in September 1939) adults and children alike listened attentively to the wireless and, in between programmes, they read and made their own entertainments.

The wireless was very popular both as a source of news and information and latterly as a provider of more general entertainment and music. For the first time ever, the familiar voices of news readers like Bruce Belfrage, John Snagge, Alvar Lidell and Freddie Grisewood became ingrained in the national consciousness, the equally recognisable tones of war correspondents like Frank Gillard, Wynford Vaughan Thomas and the incomparable Richard Dimbleby attracting listeners around the clock. Sober news gave way in the evening to slapstick and song, a new hour-long pageant of nonsense and fun, *It's That Man Again* (ITMA), starring comedian Tommy Handley becoming immensely popular. Its zany humour, idiotic buffoonery and instantly popular catch-phrases soon caught the public imagination, Handley riotously playing the 'Minister of Aggravation' in the 'Office of Twerps'. The minister was aided and abetted by Vera his secretary and the bibulous Colonel Chinstap. Another show that monopolised the dials was the Saturday night *Band Waggon* starring 'Big-Hearted' Arthur Askey, Richard 'Stinker' Murdoch, Syd Walker and Charles Smart. Musically, the nation was well catered for, the romantically stirring voices of Gracie Fields and Vera Lynn – the Forces Sweetheart – evoking as much sentiment and patriotism as the national anthem.

For younger listeners, Derek McCulloch, 'Uncle Mac', was the big attraction, his avuncular style and warm personality giving *Children's Hour* all the reassurance of the warmest comfort blanket. Not that children ever got maudlin. Out in the streets with their friends, all thoughts of war were forgotten apart from the recitation of a popularly adapted little ditty to the tune that accompanied the marching dwarfs in the popular Walt Disney cartoon:

Whistle while you work!
Hitler is a twerp,
Goering's barmy,
So's his army.
Whistle you work.

And there were always improvised games to play and the usual whip and tops, skipping ropes and marbles, Rita Millington of Sheffield recalling a particularly fine sledge made by her father:

“The area where we lived was hilly so when winter came, we would always go sledging. Mine was made from scrap pieces of wood but it was a smasher. As there was very little traffic about, we were able to sledge on roads. And there was a Barrage Balloon Depot not far from us. We would often go for a walk to see the balloons which were huge.”

Other children remembered excursions to inspect war damage, the more imaginative youngsters collecting and swapping bomb fragments and parts of aircrafts such as Perspex canopies and insignia.

After playtime, kids read the *Beano, Dandy*, *Rover*, *Knockout*, *Superman* and *Batman* comics, and lots of books featuring heroes recruited to the national cause. William Brown, the star of the *Just William* books, was enlisted to the war effort in *William and the Evacuees* and *William Does His Bit*, the legendary pilot Biggles also waving the flag in *Biggles Defies the Swastika*. For very young children, there was the prolific output of the phenomenally popular Enid Blyton who penned *Five O'Clock Tales* and *The Happy Story Book*. For older children, her books *Five on a Treasure Island*, *Five Go Adventuring Again*, *Five Run Away Together* and *Five Go to Smugglers' Top* sold by the thousands.

Adults also read with avidity but the lack of newsprint and a ban on increases in circulation restricted newspapers like the *The Times* and the *Daily Telegraph* to six or eight pages. Curtailed editions of magazines such as *Picture Post* were also in great demand, the ever popular and well-thumbed *Housewife* contracting to pocket size by 1940, to be passed on endlessly to friends and neighbours. Some new adult books were produced but numbers were severely down on prewar levels, publishers sensing the public mood in their choice of titles. The most popular volumes satisfied a yearning for a nostalgically remembered Old England of ideals and idylls, notions of what it was like to be a proud countryman of Robin Hood, Nelson, William Wilberforce, Wordsworth, Dickens and Shakespeare, being brought into ever sharper focus by imperilling Nazi ideology. Books like *English Custom and Usage* (Christina Hole, Batsford 1941), *Memories of Moor, Stream and Woodland* (D. R. H. Williams, Robert Hale 1944) and *A Little Fishing Book* (Cecil, Lord Harmsworth, Frederick Muller 1942) brought comfort and solace during the dark days, Lord Harmsworth noting the following in the rather apologetic introduction to his book:

“An odd time it may seem, with a touch of levity perhaps about it, for the publication of a book that has nothing to do with the world tragedy in which we are all involved. But the author is encouraged by the thought that, more even than in days of peace, there is a present need for recreation of the mind and spirit, and if these pages serve to lighten for an hour or so the burdens of a few war workers, they will not have been printed in vain.”

At the time, publishers, like everybody else, were motivated by patriotic instincts to ‘do their bit’ and in addition to publications about English traditions and rural topics, they produced books about horticulture, animal husbandry and do-it-yourself. Raw materials for the publishing trade were in short supply and a Book Production Economy Standard was introduced to regulate the quality of materials used in bindings.

During the war, the maxim for many was ‘Keep Your Pecker Up’, any diversion or entertainment helping to assuage and minimise the constant fear and deprivation. However, one mischievous Yorkshire whippersnapper by the name of Don Bullock from Mexborough (see entry under the heading ‘Days in the Lives of ... Schoolboys and Schoolgirls’) had the time of his life:

“There used to be seasons for things to do. In summertime, we did a lot of fishing for red breasts and sticklebacks, tackle being an elder stick, cotton line, matchstick float and a nice red worm. In winter, there seemed to be icicles hanging from every roof. It was great fun to throw snowballs up to knock them down. There were slides on almost every pavement and we always had a kind of makeshift sledge. And it was a good time for knocking on doors. All year round, there were raids (stoning each other) and games like marbles and whip and tops.

The older kids made kites using a couple of thin sticks. Crossed them X, tied them at the centre, crossed over with cotton, tied cotton round the four corners, laid them on a sheet of newspaper and cut round an inch over size, then with flour and water made a paste, applied it to the oversize edges, turned them in and stuck them down and placed in front of the fire to dry out. After drying, add about six feet of tailings. Special strong kite cotton was used on a reel to fly the kite.

Best of all for Bill and me was birds nesting. We had our own names for birds – blackbirds (blackies), thrushes (throllies), hedge sparrows (dickies), house sparrows (spuggies) and magpies (maggies).

Sometimes, we went down to wave and cheer the army convoys that passed by, shouting: 'Got any gum chum?' Another place was at a junction of the LMS (London Midland Scottish) and LNER (London North Eastern Railway) at the far end of town. Here, trains slowed or stopped and soldiers threw badges and buttons to us kids. How I wished I'd saved them.”

Chapter 2

'Dig for Victory'

For almost a decade, every sinew of production and manufacturing muscle was dedicated to the insatiable demands of the war. Even essential commodities were severely rationed, the disruption of supply lines and the loss of hundreds of thousands of tons of raw materials, oil, food and other cargoes to the depredations of surface raiders and U-boats causing chronic shortages. Faced with such hardships, farmers ploughed through the night aiming to bring an additional two million acres of land into production by the end of April 1940. And the British people joined in, growing their own food and recycling and improvising as never before. For the first time in a hundred years, the masses learnt the difference between a spade and a shovel, thousands of weed filled gardens and allotments falling under the spell of the spade and the hoe, exhortations in leaflets, radio announcements, newspapers, magazines and books urging the population to 'Dig for Victory'.

The new shoots of involvement were everywhere, railway embankments, grass verges, golf courses, tennis courts, bowling greens, recreation grounds and even window boxes all sprouting greens for the pot. No postage stamp plot was too small, books such as the *Kitchen Garden and Allotment* by T. W. Sanders providing a wealth of advice about growing techniques and yield maximisation. 'Never, previously, have such numbers of people been brought to realise the pressing need and immense importance of growing vegetables and salads to keep the home table supplied, instead of relying on the market and the shop', noted its introduction, the section on manures and fertilisers running to seven pages. Trumpeting the cause of not wasting a thing, the book expounded on the virtues of dried blood, cow, pig and horse dung, sheep and rabbit droppings, flue dust, soot, hair, hoof and horn meal, powdered oyster shells, leather dust and parings, seaweed and night soil: 'solid cesspool or dry earth-closet contents' and 'liquid sewage' all being particularly recommended for fruit trees, rhubarb, sea kale and asparagus.

Lord Woolton, the Minister of Food recommended such books urging:

> Dig! Dig! Dig!
> And your muscles will grow big.
> Keep on pushing in the spade!
> Never mind the worms,
> Just ignore the squirms,
> And when your back aches, laugh with glee,
> And keep on diggin'
> Till we give our foes a wiggin'
> Dig! Dig! Dig! to Victory.

Sanders' theme of recycling waste was further extended in the development of communal pig clubs, whole families and entire streets joining together to rear a pig fed on household scraps. By 1942, there were 4,000 pigs clubs nationwide, members taking turns in boiling up vegetable waste and leftovers to destroy bacteria and in cleaning out sties. Although it was against the rules, many pigs were killed and butchered by amateurs in makeshift abattoirs. But oh! did they taste good.

* * *

“On June 4th 1941, I met my husband Ken through my friend Betty. He was billeted at her mother's house from the army. We married on April 17th 1943. We borrowed dresses, tables and cutlery. Neighbours brought what they could from their rations for a meal. My aunt made a cake, the top made of sponge, the other tiers made of cardboard covered with white ceiling wallpaper. It looked good though!”

(Ivy Shears, Hull)

* * *

“You couldn't get make-up for love nor money during the war. Lipstick was like gold dust. If you had any odd ends left you'd crumble them into an egg cup and let it stand in a bowl of hot water till the pieces melted. Then you'd mould it and start again. To get rouge, we'd take slivers of lipstick and mix them with almond oil or cold cream. Mascara? Forget it. Burnt cork, soot or black shoe polish had to do. Nothing went to waste. After the tea was mashed, I'd keep the leaves in muslin bags for use as facemasks for me and my sister. It got so bad at times that I got to rubbing the scraped greaseproof margarine wrappers over my face. But we had to keep up appearances.”

(Margery Trobell, Brighouse)

* * *

One old chap who was only four years old when war was declared recalls his mother plying RAF personnel from a nearby camp with tea and cakes:

“In exchange, they used to bring us sweets and, if a barrage balloon had burst, some of the white bits. My mum made shopping bags out of it.”

(Paul Marshall, Hull)

* * *

“When my daughter excitedly opened a parcel I sent from my base, her face dropped in disappointment. Expecting a toy and receiving what she thought was a piece of driftwood, she threw the banana into the fire! Bananas and other foodstuffs were so rare during the war that even single fruits were auctioned and one patriotic farmer grew a field full of onions and sold the entire crop for £5,000 to buy a Spitfire.

People were encouraged to save all manner of waste and unwanted materials for the war effort. Kitchens were robbed of saucepans; chapels, bowling greens and city parks sacrificed their fences and entrance gates; wardrobes were emptied of last year's fashions; granddad Sidney had his newspaper prematurely snatched if he nodded off before completing the crossword, and even Winston lost several bones. My family led the line in salvaging anything that could be flung at the Germans, one of my sisters-in-law single-handedly equipping an airborne battalion at Arnhem. When clearing out several drawers of a dusty tallboy, Ethel – Old Parachute Knickers – discovered umpteen pairs of faded silk undergarments. In still being able to peel an orange in my pocket, I've never lost that 'Waste Not Want Not' mentality, my wife's wartime tactic of drying the skins of birthday oranges – if you could get them – for fire lighting, influencing my own fumblings with the citrus to this day. Dried orange peel, bacon rind and spent candle grease were all used in encouraging a blaze. These firelighters were laid on top of a lattice of rolled up newspapers. Double sheets would be rolled into a tube, flattened and folded in the middle at right angles, subsequent folds left and right concertina fashion creating a combustible bed for the coal. And then a match. And then another, a smouldering promise giving the hope of warmth, six Lucifer's and thirty lung-emptying blows later. Once the fire was lit, it was time to bring up the heavy artillery, the final double-spread of the *Daily Express* serving as a draught-drawer. The technique here was to carefully hold the newspaper in outstretched hands over the hearth, the sudden exclusion of air causing a sucking void in the chimney, the upward rush fanning the flames. The trick was in knowing when to withdraw the bulging paper before it was sucked up the flue. Hold it too long and a fast-creeping scorch mark would radiate from its centre threatening fingers and the entire room. If it caught fire, you had to act quickly, either crumpling it up and allowing it to fall on the fire or releasing it, risking a chimney fire. After the war, I taught my nephew James to light the fire. He was always a bit cack-handed but he survived. ”

(Frank Glusburn, Leeds)

* * *

“Rationing was never a great problem. With a large garden, we grew all our own fruit and vegetables. The only treat I ever queued for were some oranges one Christmas. Word had spread that some would be available at the fruit market near Holy Trinity Church. I hurried there during my lunch hour and to my delight was able to buy half a dozen – the maximum allowed per customer – which were shared with the family on Christmas Day. We were good friends with our Co-op butcher and on our Saturday morning visit he carefully took our coupons, but there was always an extra little parcel which found its way into our shopping bag unannounced. Our delightful little Postmistress (Miss Butler) would also sometimes knock on our door when she brought our post saying ‘I’ve brought you a few sweeties if you would like them.

Clothes were on coupons for quite some time after the end of the war but two things became available coupon-free. These were the dark grey army blankets and parachutes. My mother was an expert seamstress having been apprenticed to the well known society dressmaker Madame Clapham when she was younger. We bought two army blankets and a parachute from which mother made two tailored coats for my sister and myself and a whole variety of pyjamas, blouses and shirts for the family.”

(Peggy J. Lowthrop, Hull)

* * *

“I used to buy bones. Boil them in a big pan with a few cabbage leaves and you had a passable broth. I also gave the kids condensed milk sandwiches with a sprinkle of sugar on top.”

(Bridget Railton, Doncaster)

* * *

“One envelope makes fifty cartridge wads; sixty large cigarette cartons makes one outer shell container; one nine-inch enamelled saucepan makes a bayonet; a broken fork plus an enamelled pail makes a Tommy gun and a mixture of leaky garden hoses, old hot water bottles, rubber teapot spouts, bathing caps and golf balls would yield barrage balloons and airmen’s dinghies.”

(Article in a popular women’s magazine exhorting readers to be ‘salvage conscious’)

* * *

"I used to pinch cigs when dad was asleep. He never noticed that the odd one was missing ... but only one mind. When the war started he got called up of course and it all changed. You couldn't get cigs anywhere and in those days nobody left fag ends. They'd stick a pin in one end and bite on it, puffing away to the very end. We'd no alternative. Me and a lad in our street started experimenting with dried leaves and other such things. And we made long pipes-of-peace out of wood just like those in the cowboy films. We tried everything ... leaves, grass and shredded liquorice stick if we could get it. It's a wonder we didn't finish up with lungs like lace curtaining."

(Wilfred Spottiswood, Silsden)

* * *

"From the very beginning of the war, well over 200 Cottingham volunteers, independently and in small groups, had been knitting comforts for the men serving in the forces and, by early 1940, about 1,500 articles had already been sent to forces in the East Riding including the RAF, the Seamen's Institute, the minesweepers (mainly converted trawlers), the Red Cross and the Finland Fund. These items included socks, balaclava helmets, mittens, gloves, pullovers, hospital blankets, patchwork quilts, and hospital jackets. The volunteers watched war approaching with a feeling of helplessness and inevitability and when it came, they were determined to offer support to our forces by knitting and sewing personal gifts – a reminder that our men and women were not forgotten.

A new fund raising committee was formed and lots of organisations were involved, the committee seeking £250 by means of a direct approach to individuals and groups, a house-to-house envelope collection and a flag day. £250 equates today to about £6,000! The committee reported that in five and a half years, they had raised £660 15s 1d – equivalent now to nearly £16,000, the bulk of the spending going on wool.

One notoriously parsimonious shopkeeper gave 1d. Another small family in very straitened circumstances (at one time they tried to sell hot peas from their front door) also gave 1d, a sum that I know they could ill afford. Mrs E. M. Clapham who ran a famous fashion house – Madame Clapham's – in the city gave £1 with an apology that she couldn't send more. The Dutch residents were especially generous.

The early supplies of wool seem to have been donated by the knitters or donated to them. Wool does not appear to have been rationed at that time but it soon was and it then became a general practice to 'recycle' old garments. The same applied to cloth coats. Use of salvaged wool was not possible or adequate when quality material was required for four-ply garments in RAF blue, navy blue, khaki grey, M98 (whatever that was) and jungle green. Supplies were generally purchased from the Personal Service League in London. The Army also occasionally sent wool free of charge in exchange for knitted garments. Forty knitting book manuals were purchased at an early stage.

The operation was formally wound up in October 1945 when it was reported that 27 cwts – 2,500 miles – of wool had been knitted, the final garment tally being:

socks, 2,135 pairs – scarves, 1,391 – mittens, 696 pairs
pullovers, 362 – helmets and cap scarves, 602 pairs
gloves, 305 pairs – drivers gloves, 190 pairs
Arctic socks, 104 pairs – cuffs, 97 pairs – balaclavas, 40
Artic stockings, 70 pairs – Arctic helmets, 69
Grand total: 6,061.”

(Ian Wright, Cottingham)

* * *

“Up to 1935, urine was used commercially in Yorkshire, a textile mill in Huddersfield so valuing the liquid that it was considered criminal for employees not to donate their own voidings. On a smaller scale, urine also figured in the manufacturings of a Halifax wheelwright in the 1940s and it is thought that some enterprising mill owners collected the commodity from local POW camps.”

(From *Yorkshire Privies* by Len Markham, Countryside Books, 1996)

* * *

“My father, Leonard Thompson came from Leeds. During the war, he served with the Royal Engineers. As a trained compositor, he was seconded to the American Fifth Army's Psychological Warfare Branch printing propaganda leaflets and other literature to spread disillusionment and disaffection amongst the enemy during the Allied push through Italy. Being an ever-practical Yorkshireman, at the end of the conflict, he brought back a number of Nazi flags to Leeds, my equally practical mother producing several eye-catching red shirts and blouses for me and my brother and sisters. The cut-out swastikas became floor cloths.”

(Bernard Thompson, Arles-sur-Tech, France)

* * *

"In winter 1944, mother and me were staying a few nights with the Barstow's in their archetypal cottage in Thornhill Lees. He was a miner or a wool comber. Anyway, the war seemed to have by-passed the cottage, whereas mum and I were hardened London veterans. Late one evening, the siren went. We promptly scuttled under the table. I can still remember Mr Barstow puffing his pipe and saying to Mrs Barstow: 'Is that what they do in London then?' To which she replied: 'Yes, I think they've got to. It's the law down south.'"

(Brian Dunning, Bath)

Chapter 3

Crime and Social Ills

The war produced a peculiar set of circumstances allowing lawlessness to flourish, reported crime rising from 304,000 cases in 1939 to 478,000 cases in 1945. An explosion in legislative strictures coupled with a reduction in police numbers from 82,000 to 60,000 fuelled an escalating crime wave, the vulnerability of empty premises and lone women, the temptations offered by bombed out buildings, the blackout conditions allowing criminals to operate unseen and the huge potential profits from stolen goods whose value had been massively increased as a consequence of shortages, creating a sub culture at odds with the propagandist myth.

Burglars and looters had field days especially in blackout conditions, the siphoning off of rationed petrol from unattended cars (they had no locking petrol caps in those days) becoming a national scourge. With millions of men absent from homes left unoccupied for long periods by woman working shifts, opportunities for breaking and entering were rife, bombed out, open-to-the-sky houses presenting the easiest pickings of all. Stealing from coin-operated gas meters became a massive problem, meters ripped open by blast damage presenting opportunities galore, even otherwise law-abiding civilians such as ARP wardens falling to temptation. Hundreds of people were arrested for the offence; 90 per cent of these had no previous convictions.

Every workplace was affected by petty pilfering – long pockets, huge overcoats, capacious hats, bulging gas mask bags and maternity wear the size of marquees ('but I didn't know you were pregnant Betty?') hiding a whole range of stolen goods, searches by commissionaires at dock and factory gates doing little to stem the tide. Like smuggling in the previous century, purloining gained a certain respectability, everybody, including the clergy ('More tea vicar? Yes it is nice . . . it fell off the back of a lorry') taking advantage of wartime conditions. The cost of theft from British Railways topped £1 million in 1941 alone and losses at the ports were equally as severe, rationed commodities finding their way within a few hours onto the lucrative black market. The police struggled to cope, their depleted numbers marked by many aged officers who were long since past retirement age, hardly keeping pace with the gangs of fly young 'spivs' who operated in the twilight.

Opportunist thefts increased tenfold. Quick-witted thieves in Bradford made off with the mayoral gold chain. The Mayor and his citizens were outraged at this effrontery to civic pride and a subscription scheme was launched, members of the public donating old gold in the form of unwanted wedding rings, badges and brooches for melting down. Over twenty-eight ounces of the precious metal were subscribed and the Birmingham factory of Yorkshire based mail order firm Empire Stores was charged with making a replacement chain. However, the insatiable demand for goods – especially foodstuffs that had been easily obtainable before the war – prompted thieves and burglars to select less scintillating pickings, eschewing mayoral chains and diamond earrings for Sunday joints – 'I only turned by back for a second and he must have been in through the open door and gone,' and potato and apple crops in unattended allotments and orchards. And there were lots of unreported and unchallenged incidents of thefts like these, scarce police manpower and the petty nature of the crimes causing most people to shrug their shoulders and move on. In cases where offenders were apprehended and presented before the magistrate's courts, publicity was kept to an absolute minimum to maintain the propagandist illusion of a society totally united against the enemy with no one working against the cause.

Much of the stolen property was sold on street corners or in the bars of shady pubs but some went to legitimate shopkeepers who were scrutinised by 900 ministry inspectors keen to uncover incidents of profiteering. The making of excessive profits at the expense of customers was proscribed by the Prices of Goods Act – under its terms, a licence was required to sell canned peas – one trader having to stump up a 7 guineas (£7.7s) fine with 7 guineas costs for making an excess profit of 3½d over a four months trading period. Over charging and other scams in the retail trade were commonplace, deliberately miscalibrated weighing scales, under-the-counter sales to privileged customers and the adulteration and bulking out of goods with worthless and sometimes dangerous additives adding to the woes of purchasers. Always quick to spy opportunities for fleecing the public, some unscrupulous traders took on short leases on bomb damaged premises, crowding the windows with flashy baubles to attract customers inside where they were sold black market goods at inflated prices. Having made a killing after a few weeks trading, they promptly left before the inspectors could arrive.

Criminality in rural areas was easier to conceal. Away from the towns, it was the common practice to raise, unbeknown to the authorities, an 'illicit pig' alongside a 'legal' pig. A Farnley Tyas resident remembered that several complicit neighbours often brought scraps and crusts to the sty on the understanding that when the beast was slaughtered, they would get their share. After the killing, the animal was butchered, portioned out and wrapped in brown paper ready for delivery in a van. However, the vehicle was stopped by a policeman whose bicycle had developed a puncture on Hade Edge near the *Bay Horse* pub. He cadged a lift, immediately becoming aware of the illicit cargo. When he got back to the police station, without a word he held out his hand and received his welcome Sunday lunch.

Fuel kept the war machine running. Indispensable in taking the fight to Hitler, it was in chronically short supply, the majority of imports going for military and commercial purposes, it's rarity and high demand on the black market attracting the attention of profiteers. In an attempt to thwart the illicit trade, fuel stocks were dyed red to assist police officers in tracking down illegal use. But, as in any age, the criminal factions were one jump ahead, one enterprising gang soon discovering that the dye could be removed by passing the fuel through the air filters in surplus gas masks.

The draconian imposition of blackout regulations – it was illegal to allow the glow from a lighted cigarette to penetrate the gloom lest it act as a beacon for Luftwaffe bomb aimers – criminalized 925,000 people during the war and almost one person in fifty offended. One man was fined for lighting a match on a railway station in an attempt to cast some light on the disappearance of his false teeth. The peak year for blackout offences was 1940 when there were 300,000 prosecutions.

Although the rationing system was accepted as the cornerstone of the fight against shortages and as a loathsome necessity, abuses were rife. The forging and stealing of ration books and petrol and clothing coupons became commonplace and hard to detect, the government struggling to tighten controls. In the first year of clothes rationing, 800,000 people lost their ration books and twenty-seven million new coupons were issued, the confusion making fraud even easier. It became an offence to transfer coupons between friends even if no money changed hands and anyone who obtained goods without surrendering coupons with the cooperation of unscrupulous shopkeepers was liable to a fine. In order to further circumvent the system, some individuals adopted dual identities.

The lack of manpower in the coalfields promoted draconian measures to maintain output, the Bevin Boy initiative recruiting 21,800 extra miners. The scheme, despite the random nature of recruitment by ballot, was not universally welcomed and in March 1944 engineering apprentices in Yorkshire staged a strike, the onerous conditions imposed on raw recruits exciting vigorous debate in the House of Commons in June of that year. Some of the so called 'ballotees' refused to obey Ministry of Labour instructions to report to designated pits, one Sheffield lad suggesting that he would be better employed as an electrician. He was sentenced to three months imprisonment. There were 500 prosecutions during the first year of the scheme, 147 convicted men going to gaol.

Another severe law found its way onto the statute books. The offence of breeding disaffection among service personnel was outlawed. Suggestions that soldiers were jingoistic fools to put their lives on the line and fight for a country that only paid them a pittance compared, for example, with munitions workers, was tantamount to treason.

Other than blackout infringements, the most universally perpetrated crime of the war years was probably black marketeering, nearly every person in the country technically falling foul of the onerous regulations at some time during the conflict. Every commodity in short supply was traded illegally. Especially at Christmas, there was a ready demand for toys made in clandestine workshops from materials smuggled from factories, Scarce meat supplies encouraged unscrupulous farmers to slaughter diseased, old or sub-standard animals for human consumption risking public health.

Constant strain, sleep deprivation, binge drinking, disruptions in family life and widespread infidelities put immense pressures on personal relationships during the war years leading to hundreds of disputes, fights and domestic murders. Expedited arrests, trials and executions were the order of the day, Trevor Elvin, a twenty-one-year-old glassworker's fitter typically going to the gallows on 10 September 1943 in Armley Gaol in Leeds a few months after murdering Cudworth Land Army girlfriend Violet Wakefield in a fairground dodgem enclosure in Barnsley. A petition was signed by 38,178 local people and the life of the condemned man was championed by Barnsley MP Frank Collindridge, but Home Secretary Herbert Morrison affirmed the verdict rejecting pleas that the victim had 'done him wrong' by carrying on another relationship.

One of the most imaginative and profitable criminal activities of all was currency fraud. In liberated France, £1 sterling could yield 500 FF on the black market – more than 2½ times the official exchange rate. Quick to capitalise, crooks went over to Paris with wads of notes, buying a Pandora's Box of liqueurs, wines, perfumes, silk stockings and other luxury goods for retailing back in England at a vast profit.

Between 1939 and 1945, there was a four-fold increase in the number of divorce petitions filed for adultery, 58 per cent of the petitions being lodged by men. Although the number of marriages reached an all time high in 1940, births plunged to a record low in 1941 and there were volubly expressed fears 'this is no world for children!' – of a rapidly reducing population dominated by old people. Illegitimate births were 4.4 per cent in 1939; by 1945, this had rocketed to 9.1 per cent.

Chapter 4
Tragedies

❝On the night of 17th March 1945, my mother and two brothers aged nine and thirteen were at the Astoria Cinema in Hull. It was a treat for them. The warning came up on the screen that there was an air raid in progress. They left the cinema and waited in a queue for a tram. When it arrived they were pushed further back and had to wait for the next one. Consequently, by the time they got to Sherburn Street – we lived down Rosemead Street – the bombs started dropping but because the war was nearly finished, the shelters were locked. As the bombs came down, a man, who was watching the raid on his doorstep, threw himself on my brothers to protect them. Unfortunately, all three were killed and my sister and mother were seriously injured. My mother was three months pregnant at the time. My mother and sister survived but my sister, till the day she died, lived with a large piece of shrapnel in her chest. It was in such a position that an operation was out of the question. My mother was scarred for life because of the amount of shrapnel in her body. At the time of the raid, I'd just got home from the Regal Cinema. The ironical thing is that the raid was the last one of the war and my brothers and myself were evacuated twice but still managed to be at home for the worst air raid of all. I still find it traumatic to talk about it.❞

(Mrs J. Bedforth, Hull)

* * *

❝Wakefield was attacked by the Luftwaffe on 28 August 1940, bombs falling on Norton Street, Belle Vue, injuring four people and destroying six houses. The worst attack of the war came on the night of 14 March 1941, two bombs hitting Thornes Road, killing six residents and injuring four more. Explosions damaged or destroyed scores of houses, ARP crews dousing the flames with water pumped from the Calder River in a show of preparedness.❞

* * *

❝Our house suffered a direct hit and was rendered uninhabitable. The following morning, a bomb damaged double-decker bus was despatched to collect the family and other survivors. I can remember granny moaning about the draught from the bus door which was open and me saying to mother that I can't understand granny complaining about the draught from the open door as there were no windows left in the bus and mother telling me to shut up as we would never hear the end of it.❞

(Testimony of Anita Morfit of Hull, who was five years old at the time of the raid on the family home in South Boulevard, Hessle Road, Hull)

* * *

During the infamous Sheffield Blitz on the night of the 12 December 1940, seventy people died in one of the worst incidents of the war, a massive bomb scoring a direct hit on the seven-storey *Marples Hotel* in the city centre. Not even its walls were left standing. Half the victims were women. All had been cowering in the cellar. Seven survivors were rescued from the rubble next day but such was the carnage, that only fourteen bodies were ever identified.

* * *

Tragedy struck the sleepy hamlet of Spaunton near Lastingham and the North York Moors in October 1943. On an operational sortie to a target in Germany, a fully ladened RAF bomber crashed in the village, destroying a cottage and the blacksmith's forge. Alerted by the plight of the aircraft, the unlucky tenant of Manor Farm was killed as he went to investigate, a passage door blowing off in his face.

* * *

On the early evening of 14 November 1944, a Halifax bomber on an internal training flight from RAF Snaith developed engine trouble. It plummeted to the ground and crashed at Tingley near Leeds killing all seven crewmen. The crash was witnessed by a traumatised thirteen-year-old boy, Walter Townend from nearby East Ardsley, who in 1989 erected a memorial to the dead near the point of impact.

* * *

In one of Yorkshire's worse losses of life of the entire war, forty-nine workers – mostly women and young girls – died as fire swept through Booth's Mill in Huddersfield, in October 1941. The blaze was not a consequence of bombing but was attributed to a carelessly left pipe smouldering in a pocket. A memorial in Edgerton cemetery marks the grave of forty-four of the victims.

* * *

On 10 May 1944, a bomber crashed into a church in Selby, killing seven crew members and eight civilians.

* * *

On the evening of 14 September 1941, a twenty-five-year-old woman who was out for an evening stroll was shot dead by sentries near Scarborough beach after failing to heed a warning.

* * *

As a consequence of the blackout, more people died on Britain's roads during the first few months of the war than were killed on active service. From September to December 1939, the death toll was 4,133, an increase of 65 per cent on the corresponding figure for 1938.

* * *

On 5 March 1945, a Halifax Mk.VII bomber flying from its base at Linton-on-Ouse, fell from the sky in freezing fog. Part of a sortie of fourteen aircraft bound for Germany, the aircraft laboured under its heavy load of bombs and fuel, severe icing causing it to stall, plummet to the ground and disintegrate only twenty-one minutes after take-off. The fuselage hit properties in Nunthorpe Grove, York and an engine penetrated Nunthorpe Secondary School kitchen. The pilot and all crew members except one were killed, wireless operator/air gunner Pilot Officer J. Low bailing out just before impact. At so low an altitude, death was almost certain, but miraculously, the updraught of the exploding aircraft allowed his parachute to deploy. The airman hit a shed roof and was badly injured. There were five civilian fatalities and a further eighteen people were injured.

Chapter 5

'You're 'aving a Laugh!'

A criminal housewife was fined in the Magistrates' Court after admitting to a charge of ironing in the dark with a defective iron. Although the curtains were drawn at the time, a pilot light flashed on and off, alerting a passing ARP Warden.

* * *

F. R. Poole of No. 4 Platoon Grassington Company in Buckden wrote to *The Times* on 23 August 1940 about previously published correspondence by a disgruntled fellow member of the Home Guard who complained about the meagre five hour subsistence allowance of 1s 6d paid to service personnel. An irritated Poole concludes his letter by saying that despite the inclement northern weather, broken sleep and other discomforts, the only grouse ever heard in Yorkshire were on the adjacent moors.

* * *

A St John's Ambulance Brigade nurse recalls a posting to the sleepy hamlet of Nun Monkton near York, its elegant priory becoming a fifty-bed hospital after its sale by owner Captain Whitworth to the Red Cross. Her biggest shock was in discovering the twenty black faces of recruits newly arrived from Jamaica, all the men promptly falling down with flu. A garden party was held on the elegant lawns sweeping down to the river Ouse, coconut shy targets becoming the faces of Hitler and Mussolini. Afterwards, several wags who were clearly on the way to recovery, made an unseasonable Guy Fawkes, hoping to frighten the nurse on her nightly rounds. Sitting at the foot of a patient's bed in the mode of reading a book with a scudding moon lime lighting his moustache, the effigy of the Fuehrer is said to have looked very real.

* * *

The Luftwaffe unleashed its might on the Hall Bower area of Huddersfield on 29 August 1940. The attack slightly damaged several houses, blew several irate residents out of bed and ruined Mrs O'Shea's jam tarts!

* * *

"I was sent to Filey while I was waiting for the overseas posting and a strange thing happened there. Filey at that time (1942) was the number one training camp for the Royal Air Force Regiment and they used grounds that used to be the Butlin's Holiday Camp. The swimming pools had been made into parade grounds – all cemented and everything – and the ranges were on top of the cliffs. Anyway, we got a message that the *Gneissenau* and the *Scharnhorst*, which were two of Germany's big battleships, had broken out of port and were steaming past. So we had to put detonators in our hand grenades and the RAF Regiment had to stand on the cliffs at Filey and Flamborough Head and, as the two battleships went past, throw their grenades at the ships. I've never heard anything so daft, but, of course, we had to do it. ”

(Ken Allinson, Ferryhill, near Hartlepool)

* * *

Thoroughly inconvenienced by a war that had consigned her Rolls Royce to the garage, a self-important lady accosted a bus driver in Skipton with the words: 'Are there any seats on this bus?' the driver nonchalantly replying, 'Yes madam ... but they're all full.'

* * *

“For a woman not being able to cook, is like impotence in a man. ”

(Remark attributed to a ravenous unidentified Huddersfield man – identification was impossible following repeated blows from a rolling pin – after greeting his wife, who had just completed an eight-hour shift filling tank shells with high explosive)

* * *

On 13 June 1940, the government banned the ringing of church bells except in the event of invasion, the imposition of this campanological early warning system attracting ridicule and scorn. Someone pointed out that the enemy might deliberately attack churches as a legitimate military target, congregations everywhere complaining at the loss of their daily call to service. The ban was eventually lifted on 4 April 1943, no less than Winston Churchill observing: 'For myself, I cannot help feeling that anything like a serious invasion would be bound to leak out!'

* * *

In the journals of famous weather guru Bill Foggitt of Thirsk, a January 1940 entry records an all time low temperature of 28 degrees of frost. Parts of the Humber froze over and ice floes drifted downstream accumulating as pack ice under the Victoria Pier in Hull. Bill's celebrated prognosticating pine cone was shut up tight for weeks.

* * *

"Why am I black? Well, I'm a US Army spy son. This here colour is camouflage for when we're operating at night. But when I get stateside, I'll have an injection. Then I'll be a white boy just like you."

(GI's response to an enquiry from Yorkshire schoolboy amazed at seeing his first black soldier)

* * *

"I was passing a barbershop and it was all boarded up from the bombing during the previous night. Chalked on the window boards were the words: 'WE'RE OPEN! COME INSIDE FOR A SHAVE AS CLOSE AS WE HAD LAST NIGHT'."

(Peggy Callaghan, Hull)

* * *

"The Germans will never conquer Yorkshire. They'll starve to death in a week. With accents like theirs, they'll never be issued with ration books."

(A. Sleights, Scarborough)

* * *

"That dame smells."

(Remark made by a GI at a dance in Wetherby. But what could a girl do whose patriotic duty was to restrict bathing to no more than once a week in just five inches of water ... often without soap? She could ensure less odorous clinches by adopting a tactic recommended by a popular magazine – patting bicarbonate of soda powder under the armpits)

* * *

Mass Observation – a continuing wartime survey of habits and attitudes – came up with a list of the nation's favourite activities. In a descending order of popularity these were:

- Staying in
- Reading
- Going to bed early
- Listening to the wireless
- Going to pubs
- Playing cards and other games
- Writing
- Smoking

* * *

❝My old Uncle Sam was a marvellous storyteller! History had no boundaries for him – he was like a time traveller. He'd fought in every war since the Battle of Hastings and always on the winning side. I believed every word he told me, and to this day, I still prefer his version of historical events.

My favourite story is the one he told me of his part in the D-Day Landings. He said he got a message that Winston Churchill wanted to see him urgently. He'd gone to London the very next day in his plane explaining that he and Winston had gone to school together and had kept in touch ever since. As soon as Winston saw him, he said 'I'm pleased to see thee Sam. We're in a spot of bother about where to launch our D-Day Landings and you could be just the man to sort it out for us.'

'Well. I can tell thee now,' said Uncle Sam, 'It's got to be Normandy. I'll tell thi what I'll do. I'll pop over tomorrow in my Spitfire and take some pictures of all the beaches and then I'll sort out a plan of invasion for thi.'

So next morning, Uncle Sam set off in his Spitfire. He was loaded down with camera equipment so he hadn't any room for weapons. He flew up and down the beaches of Normandy taking all the pictures he required and then he turned for home. He was about halfway back, flying nice and steady in second gear and eating his snap (a pork pie and half a pound of tripe) when he glanced in his mirror and there behind him was a squadron of Messerschmitts!

With no weapons, he couldn't turn and fight so he put his foot down and flew off. Then he spotted a cloud to his right so he turned quickly, dodged behind the cloud, switched his engine off and waited. The trick worked! The enemy flew straight past. Uncle Sam delivered the photos to Winston and spent an hour with him sorting out invasion plans. He cadged a couple of cigars and flew back to base.

I asked: 'Didn't you get a medal for that Uncle Sam?' He said: 'Yes I did – but it's too big to wear. It's round the back. I use it as a dustbin lid!'❞

(Walt Bywater, Barnsley – this letter first appeared in a special supplement of the *Barnsley Chronicle*: *Barnsley at War*, 1 September 1989)

* * *

❝As an evacuee, I'd come all that way by train and I were bloody starving. The man at the station says to me: 'Ey up lad. Stick that in yer gob. My treat!' It were an Oxo cube.❞

(Duke Linstead, Skipton)

* * *

"I would like to tell you of an amusing incident that happened to me during the Second World War. I was desperate for the loo, which was at the top of our garden on Scarborough Road, Foxholes. As I sat, incendiary bombs were dropped behind Foxholes Manor and a piece of shrapnel landed nearly in my lap. I bent down to pick it up and promptly got my fingers burnt."

(J. Windrass, Foxholes)

* * *

"'It looks like rain,' said the landlord putting a frothing pint down on a Dales pub counter.'That's right', replied the customer, 'I didn't think it was beer.'"

(Popular wartime drinkers joke in allusion to watered down beer)

* * *

- Don't tell the family what the dish is made from until they've tasted – and liked – it.
- Don't moan about the food you couldn't get before you serve what you could get.
- Do praise your cooking in advance to encourage their appetites.
- Do talk pleasant small talk at each meal.
- Don't mention the gas bill until everyone has finished.

(Recipe for harmonious meals published by *Mother and Home* magazine in 1940 as rationing began to bite)

* * *

Operating from occupied territories, the Germans set up a propagandist radio network called the New British Broadcasting Station purporting to represent patriotic but disillusioned Britons who were anxious to end the war. On 9 August 1940, it was soberly announced that an invasion force of 10,000 planes would imminently fly to England carrying 100,000 paratroopers disguised as British troops wearing uniforms left by the BEF in France. To add to the confusion, without a titter, the communiqué added that some of the invaders would be dressed as miners.

* * *

"It's a nice day for the war."

(Casual greeting overheard on a bus in Cleckheaton in April 1941)

* * *

If, after listening to the nine o'clock news on the radio on 29 October 1939, you were feeling down ... this reflection on country life written by a ten year old evacuee might have cheered you up:

"The cow is a mammal. It has six sides, right, left, an upper and below. At the back it has a tail, on which hangs a brush. With this it sends the flies away so that they do not fall into the milk. The head is for the purpose of growing horns and so that the mouth can be somewhere. The horns are to butt with, and the mouth is to moo with. Under the cow hangs the milk. It is arranged for milking. When people milk, the milk comes and there is never an end to the supply. How the cow does it I have not yet realised but it makes more and more. The cow has a fine sense of smell, and one can smell it far away. This is the reason for the fresh air in the country. The man cow is called an ox. It is not a mammal. The cow does not eat much, but what it eats, it eats twice so that it gets enough. When it is hungry it moos and when it says nothing it is because its inside is full up with grass."

* * *

"Take your hand off my knee. No! Not you. You!"

(Admonishment of a pretty girl in a packed, blacked-out train compartment in Huddersfield)

* * *

Two soldiers indicted for murder turned glumly from the dock after being sentenced to death. Both men were bawled out by an escorting police officer for leaving their gas masks behind.

* * *

I'M BRITISH AND THE MONKEY IS FROM INDIA

(Street sign displayed on the instrument of a Leeds organ grinder after anti-Italian riots following the declaration of war by Mussolini on 10 June 1940)

* * *

"I read somewhere that one old chap complained after being rationed to five sheets of toilet paper every forty-eight hours. Toilet paper? We'd never even heard of toilet paper in our street. We made do with torn up bits of newspapers threaded on a string behind the privy door. The bits that showed pictures of Hitler and his gang were our favourites."

(Ted Flowers, Ilkley)

* * *

"Dad told me he was a firewatcher. Well, it was obvious. He stared into the flames every night and usually fell asleep."

(Edna Mountfield, Northallerton – aged six at the time)

* * *

Severe rationing had a beneficial effect in the kitchen, tongue-licked plates requiring minimal washing up. Hardly any morsel of food was wasted although pig bins were provided on many street corners as receptacles for indigestible scraps. The bins were scraped through by eagle-eyed monitors to ensure that delicacies such as bread crusts, bacon fat and apple cores were not being wasted, the more keener officials assembling incriminating evidence, gathering corroborative testimonies from local residents and staking out bins at night to catch offenders sticky-handed.

* * *

The term 'a quick flash' was coined in blacked-out red light districts, prostitutes in white mackintoshes advertising their wares by momentarily flashing torches.

* * *

"Learn to get used to it. Eels get used to skinning."

(Winston Churchill commenting after an air raid in June 1940)

* * *

"If the night is a little misty, the first big battle on English soil will probably be fought between the British Army and the LDV."

(Anonymous army officer, 6 July 1940)

* * *

"Sales of beer in this country yield the Chancellor of the Exchequer £256,000 a day. The daily cost of the war is £6 million so that one serviceman in twenty-four is being clothed, equipped, fed and paid for out of the beer duty and one aircraft in twenty-four is also being built at the expense of the beer drinker. A man may spend far more money on new clothes or a wireless set and bring no grist to the financial mill . . . beer drinkers are carrying the major burden of the cost of the war."

(Article in *Brewers Journal*)

* * *

In 1942, the regulation-ratchet tightened even further, the Government decreeing that paper wastage constituted a criminal offence. A bemused Lord Wharncliffe of Wortley Hall, Sheffield, wrote to a national newspaper complaining about the measure, suggesting consistency and uniformity in the application of the measure. Applying for a grant from the West Riding Agricultural Committee to install drains on his farm, he noted the receipt of a nine-sheeted foolscap questionnaire at a time when the careless tossing away of a bus ticket could lead to arrest. O. Mordant Burrows of Doncaster sniped to the newspaper in similar vein pointing out that 600 tons of paper pulp were being saved annually as a consequence of printing smaller and thinner bus tickets. The recently sanctioned reintroduction of flat racing would, he argued, consume the saving in the provision of race cards and bookmakers' slips.

* * *

“I object to fire-watching as it appears to me to be an attempt to pervert the fulfilment of the scripture which says that the world would be destroyed by fire.”

(Conscientious objector explaining to a tribunal why he had refused an instruction to become a firewatcher)

* * *

Yorkshire villager to Sheffield evacuee – ‘And where do you come from little boy? Evacuee to villager – ‘I'm from England mister.’

* * *

VERY WIDE OPEN
PLENTY OF BLASTED BOOKS

(Sign outside a bombed-out bookshop)

* * *

With hand grenades in short supply, one enterprising Home Guard platoon invented an organic but potentially deadly alternative – potatoes cunningly concealing razor blades. In field trials, the devices proved to be lethal in Irish Stew.

* * *

“I was just passing the fuel store your Honour and I needed a few drops of petrol to refill my cigarette lighter. I turned the tap but it just kept on coming. I was like the Sorcerer's Apprentice. I couldn't stop it so I grabbed a large container and filled it up. I wouldn't have dreamed of pinching it . . . honest. ”

(Evidence given in court by a man on trial for the theft of 500 gallons of fuel. The judge was unimpressed with the explanation and sentenced the accused to twelve months' imprisonment with hard labour)

* * *

“It was highly appropriate that I had a picture of the Fuhrer in our privy-shed, it being eminently the best place for pulling faces. With a nail through his head he awaited an Allied victory. I remember that Stalingrad afforded me the most satisfying wipe I ever had. ”

(J. Z. Smithson, Bradford)

* * *

Nineteen-year-old Halifax teenager Leslie Bowling joined local landscape gardening firm Conway's based in Commercial Street hoping for a quiet life pricking out seedlings and planting trees. Little realising that his horticultural skills would be enlisted in the war effort, he was surprised to be sent to RAF Linton-on-Ouse where he was required to camouflage the base to make it look like a garden. He helped turf the roofs of buildings, plant flowers and install crazy paving in the hope that the Luftwaffe would overlook the Lysanders and Blenheim Bombers. The technique was used all over Yorkshire.

* * *

A young man whose weakness was liquor,
Said, 'I don't like old Hitler's swastika.
He toasted its fall and dribbled, 'Cig Hall . . .
It's future is certainly bleaker'.

* * *

“I was evacuated with another lad to a family in Market Weighton. In the holidays, we liked to help out on a local farm. That's where we found out all about sex. One September, Wilf and me went to a dance. We watched one of the experienced farm hands waltzing round with a woman. He couldn't half pull 'em but that night he had a puzzled look on his face. Afterwards we asked him what was wrong. 'Nowt was wrong,' he said with a wink. 'I was just weighing things up like and wondered about her knickers. Did they have elastic round t'top or buttons down t'side?' ”

(Archie Syemonds, Richmond)

* * *

One evacuee city boy stood mesmerised as a farmer harvested a crop of potatoes and asked: 'Did you hide them down there to stop 'em been pinched in the war?'

* * *

"A bison is something to be sick into."

(Scribble on the side of a new Wakefield-manufactured landing craft as it left the factory)

* * *

"We shall defend our island home and outlive the menace of tyranny ... we shall go on to the end. We shall defend our island whatever the cost may be... we shall fight on the beaches, we shall fight in the fields and streets, we shall fight in the hills, we shall never surrender ... **and beat the buggars about the head with bottles: that's all we've got.**"

(Prime Minister Winston Churchill delivered this stirring oratory to the House of Commons in May 1940 after the debacle at Dunkirk. The un-statesmanlike comment at the end was allegedly made with a drop of the head and a whisper and was not recorded by the stenographers of *Hansard*).

* * *

In Yorkshire's last game before war broke out, Len Hutton scored a marvellous century and a single in his second innings in his side's nine-wicket win over Sussex at Hove.

* * *

"Here we have Sunday dinner every day!"

(Exuberant extract from a Yorkshire child evacuee's letter home. The author is reputed to have gained 7 lbs in one week)

* * *

Flummoxed by a war shortage of flue rods, one enterprising Keighley chimney sweep introduced a novel method of removing soot. Climbing onto roofs with a broad winged rooster, he would fasten weights to the bird's legs, lowering it down the orifice on a string. The bird would flap about causing an avalanche of soot, contained, at the front-parlour end, by a draped sack. At the end of the week, the luckless flapper was served up as smoked chicken.

* * *

George Fowler was a signalman on the Woodhead Line near Penistone during the war. Sentinel of the Woodhead Tunnel – one of the most hadean and mist-shrouded portals in the entire railway network – George was assisted in his work by a lookout man. Lacking a telephone, with only an unreliable timetable for guidance, George, at the appointed hour, had to walk to the signal carrying a wooden ladder as the integral means of ascending to the signal top was badly corroded and dangerous to climb. The bottom of the ladder was placed in the middle of the track, an alert George climbing to operate the signal. His lookout meanwhile waved a paraffin warning-lamp, its billowing smoke reducing visibility to six feet. According to George, the only certain method of anticipating the arrival of a train was by an instinctive familiarity with air displacement. Aware of a telltale breeze, he would instantly descend from his perch and throw the ladder between the tracks, the express thundering by at sixty miles per hour as he and his lookout jumped to safety.

* * *

Baked Thrushes

Ingredients

Thrushes (one for each person)
Tomatoes (peeled and chopped)
Garlic (one crushed clove)
½ cup of olives (optional)
Fat or butter
One onion (chopped)
Seasoning
Bacon (or oiled paper)

Method

Hang the thrushes for three to six days. Remove feathers and gut the birds. Brown in fat or butter in the frying pan and add the other ingredients cooking for a few minutes.Wrap in bacon (or oiled paper) and bake in a hot oven for twenty minutes.

(Wartime recipe in a popular magazine)

* * *

“We had an Anderson shelter installed halfway down our long garden and we became very familiar with every inch of it over the next two or three years. It was dark and dreary and, as I slept on the top bunk, the condensation on the undulating ridges was far too close. If you happened to turn over it was not pleasant to the touch. We spent a lot of nights in there when the raids were very bad. Grandma who suffered from a delicate chest had a liking for boiled onions! This along with the Wintergreen ointment that she rubbed on her chest left a lasting impression on all of us.”

(Jean Mary Wright, Cottingham)

* * *

On the night of the devastating Baedeker Raid on York (28/29 April 1942) when scores of people were killed and injured and over 9,500 premises were damaged, one of the main city centre bomb shelters was locked shut. A note on its door read: ‘Key On Other Door.’ The key was in fact in an unbroken glass case on the end of the shelter.

* * *

On VE Day (Tuesday 8 May 1945) everything was up for grabs. People danced and lit bonfires, strangers hugged and kissed, soldiers climbed on vehicles and sang triumphant songs, publicans handed out free beer and Hull trawlerman Walter ‘Dillinger’ Denton jumped over a store counter and started throwing clothes and fishing gear to his mates with the words: ‘There you are lads! We shouldn’t have to pay for these now.’ The celebration issue of the *Daily Mirror* was also in party mood, cartoon pin-up girl Jane daringly showing a half-revealed right breast to a shocked nation for the first time.

Chapter 6

Days in the Lives of . . .

Probably the most famous Yorkshire civilian during World War Two was Edward Frederick Lindley Wood, First Baron Irwin and Third Viscount Halifax, although even he would not have been allowed to play cricket for his county having been born in Devon's Powderham Castle in 1881. During the Great War, however, he put down his Yorkshire roots, enlisting in the Yorkshire Dragoons, residing later at Garrowby Hall near Bishop Wilton, east of York and becoming the Master of the Middleton Hunt.

Halifax was the Viceroy of India between 1926 and 1931 and an influential Conservative MP with a worldwide reputation for astute diplomacy. Becoming the principal architect of appeasement in Chamberlain's government, he made a famous visit to discuss simmering international relations with German Chancellor Hitler at Berchtesgaden on 19 November 1937. According to some reports, the normally impeccably mannered envoy almost precipitated a premature start to the war by handing his coat to the diminutive dictator believing him to be a lowly footman. The meeting went from bad to worse, the Fuehrer ranting to his guest about the calumnies uttered against the Reich by the British Parliament and its poodle press. Unimpressed, Halifax replied: 'If this is your idea of what must be done, I think I have wasted my time and yours.'

Prime Minister Chamberlain appointed Halifax Foreign Secretary after the resignation of Anthony Eden but he was effectively sidelined by new premier Winston Churchill, becoming Ambassador to Washington in 1941.

Speaking about the long-resisted Second World War, he famously said: 'I often think how much easier the world would have been to manage if Herr Hitler and Signor Mussolini had been to Oxford.'

Internationally celebrated politicians like Lord Halifax and Chamberlain were reluctant players in the deadly game of conquest and annihilation. Finally though, when the die was cast, the lot fell to ordinary men and women – combatants and civilians like the ones whose memories are recorded here – to pick up the pieces.

. . . COAL MINERS

Coal mining was always a hazardous occupation but the normal dangers were massively aggravated during wartime by a number of factors including the recruitment of unskilled and inexperienced young men and boys, the compulsory conscription of prisoners of war whose language skills were non existent or poor; and the drive to produce ever increasing tonnages sometimes from geologically difficult pits, often at the expense of safety and maintenance considerations.

The lifeblood of industry and the heart of the war machine, coal was the most vital of war commodities but by May 1941 it was obvious that the nationwide workforce of 760,000 miners could not accommodate demands. It was decided that an additional 50,000 men would be required to halt the haemorrhage of labour to the armed forces and other war industries but, over the months, various initiatives failed to significantly increase numbers, member of the War Cabinet and Minister of Labour and National Service, Ernest Bevin proposing a radical solution in the House of Commons on 2 December 1943.

It was decided that selected men between eighteen and twenty-five years of age, on becoming available for call up to the armed forces, would be conscripted into the mining industry. Selection was to be by secret ballots. These would be periodically held at times of regional labour shortages, and numbers would be randomly chosen from 0 to 9, those men whose National Service Registration Certificate registrations ended in the drawn numbers automatically going to a designated pit. The scheme was arbitrary but fair, willowy college boys from the south of England taking their places alongside front-row forward types from Yorkshire.

Two famous Yorkshire Tykes were Bevin Boys in their youth. Brian Rix actually volunteered for the scheme but Jimmy Savile, who was born in 1926, was conscripted to work in South Kirkby and Waterloo collieries. 'I went down as a boy and came up as a man,' he said of his experiences years later.

The following is a facsimile of a note delivered to bewildered raw recruits from London:

NORTH EASTERN REGION

PRINCE OF WALES COLLIERY PONTEFRACT

Trainees travel by train depart St. Pancras 10.00 am arrive Pontefract (Baghill Station) 4.37 pm, change at Sheffield.

Men should assemble at top of No. 6 Platform at 9.15 am and look out for Reception Officer with armlet.

Accommodation was in private homes or in purpose-built Miners' Hostels, Nissan huts each with twelve beds and lockers, separate toilets and showers and a central welfare block providing for every need. Recruits were allocated four blankets, three sheets, three pillow slips, three towels, a safety helmet, overalls, steel capped boots, gym shoes, vests and a padlock and key. At the end of a four-week training period, they were allowed to retain the safety helmet and boots.

There were Miners' Hostels in Barnsley, Bentley, Castleford, Doncaster, Maltby, Mexborough, Rotherham and Wakefield providing places for thousands of trainees. There was an over provision of such places, some of the hostels eventually being occupied by evacuees and displaced persons. In total there were 120 pits in South Yorkshire, 100 pits in the West Riding and 9 pits in the North Riding employing nearly 140,000 men.

Life in the mines was hazardous and unpleasant for many of the young conscripts, an accident at Hatfield Main on 12 December 1939 portending the horrors ahead. On that fateful day, an over-wind in No. 2 Shaft sent a packed cage hurtling to the bottom of the mine. Almost seventy men and boys were seriously injured and one man died. Ten miners had limbs amputated. The youngest of these was fifteen-year-old Billy Pilkington who lost his right leg.

The recruitment scheme continued until VE Day, a total of 21,800 Bevin Boys becoming miners. Despite their initial reluctance, many workers elected to stay in the industry. Many ex-miners continue to live in the Yorkshire communities they served despite the near total annihilation of their industry, only commemorative plaques marking the sites of once busy winding houses. Decades on, conversations over a pint in local working men's clubs and institutes recall memories like these:

“I started at the pit on September 4th 1939. I started sticking motties on tubs. My bloody tongue! One shift I stuck on 1200 and odd.”

“When the war started, a lot of shopkeepers, boxing managers and the like came to the pit to get out of going into the army. They were usually useless. One man had a quarry on the surface. All his blue-eyed men used to work there when they should have been on the face.”

“There was this bloke who lived on his own. He never took any snap to work. We used to drop spice on the floor so that he could find them. We told him they had dropped through the cracks in the pit from the sweet factory.”

Name: Harold Jackson
Born: 19 August 1925
Wartime location: Hull and Doncaster

"I was born in Beverley but later moved to Hull. When I was thirteen years old, mother died and we more or less had to fend for ourselves. I left school at fourteen. My ambition was to go as a deck hand on a trawler. On a Sunday morning we'd walk down to the fish docks and see all the boats coming in ready for the market; also the boats going out on an evening to the fishing grounds. It really fascinated me.

My stepmother looked after us but she was not the best of persons and ruled with a rod of iron. It was 7s 6d a week as a deck hand so I went as an errand boy to the Colonial Stores for 10s 6d. After two years, I went to work in a dairy at Leconfield, working twelve hours a day seven days a week delivering milk in a van to Beverley.

I had a medical for the Army on 3 November 1943 and found myself on my way to Doncaster on 24 January 1944 on a 7s 6d travel warrant to Askern colliery. When the ballot for Bevin Boys came out, my number came up. You had to go where you were sent or you could go to prison. I was eighteen or nineteen and I wasn't very happy especially after loosing mother and not having much of a life. And I got no help from my aunts.

My stepmother saw me off at Hull Paragon. I went with Little Tommy. We got to Askern and reported to the Miners' Welfare. There we were kitted up with a pair of boots and a safety helmet but we had to use our own clothing. On the second day, we went down Askern to look around. When we got on the chair, there was this big banksman* – around eighteen stone. We held on to the handrail like grim death – about thirty of us. A lever was pulled and we set off. My heart went bump and we finally made it to the bottom. It was very warm and pleasant and we had a walk round and a little lecture from our instructor. We didn't see a coalface.

I lodged in Doncaster. We got £3 a week and had to pay £1 1s board. The rest was for bus fares and odd items such as Brylcreem, toothpaste and razor blades. I was the only lodger, sharing my room with the landlady's young son. I didn't feel homesick. The landlady put up my snap and cooked breakfast. I was well looked after.

I spent a little time in the lamp room to begin with and when a few more Bevin Boys arrived, we were given mundane jobs on the pit top. The other miners treated us quite well although there were some remarks as some thought we were conscientious objectors which we weren't.

After six weeks training, I went to Yorkshire Main in March 1944. Underground, it was different to Askern. It was more up to date; more modern. I was loading coal off the conveyors into tubs. I came out in September 1947.”

* Banksman, the man in charge of the surface cage.

(From Brian Elliott's *Pit Voices* oral history project)

Name: George Hurst
Born: 25 September 1924
Wartime location: Bolton-upon-Dearne

“I was fourteen when I left school in 1938. I couldn't get a job so I spent six months at what we called the 'Dole' school at Mexborough ... but I couldn't get an apprenticeship. They were setting lads on at Barnburgh Main and dad told me I could go to the pit but had only to work on the pit top. I started on the screens*. I worked on the screens until I was seventeen and a half years old in 1941 when I had to register for the armed forces. I was called into the manager's office and he told me I had to go down the pit. I said I didn't want to, but I was told I'd be sent to goal for six months and would have to go down the pit afterwards. I decided I didn't want to be in goal so I went down the pit. At the time, they started bringing Bevin Boys in as they were so short of men.

My first job was as a pony driver. I was told to go and get a pony. I was dealing with loaded tubs and taking empties to tub stalls. There was Old Sam and Bonnie. When Old Sam retired, a bloke bought him for ten bob and kept him as a pet. Some of the ponies knew when they had more than two tubs on. They wouldn't move! They could hear you putting the links on.

I always had bread and dripping for my snap and perhaps, on one day, bread and jam. When I first started work, on the first day, dad got up with me and cooked me bacon and egg and tomato and he told me that was the first time and the last! I used to leave the house at five for a six o'clock start. I was pony driving for about six months.

After pony driving, I went on haulage work, knocking coal on and lashing on and knocking empties off, doing that job until I was about twenty-two. That's when I went training to go on the coalface. We got a day wage when training. I went back to the Barnsley Bed when my training had finished. We earned about 32 or 33 shillings a day. I did this until I was about twenty-five years old.”

* Pit top areas where waste material was separated from the coal and where the coal was graded, both by hand and mechanical riddles. Screening was usually the reserve of boys, the old or partly disabled miners.

(From *Yorkshire Mining Veterans*, Brian Elliott, Wharncliffe Publishing, 2005)

Doncaster Amalgamated Collieries Ltd. S.D. **Form 4**

REVISED SAFETY INSTRUCTIONS TO BOYS. CARD 4.
PONY HAULAGE

I HAVE BEEN SHOWN HOW

- To approach a pony when in the stables.
- To harness and unharness my pony.
- To limber him up or use Sling Gears.
- To attach him to or detach him from tubs using a Cotter pin for limbers.
- To pass through doors or cloths with pony and tub so as not to cause any interference with ventilation and to report any damage that may be done.
- To use the Safety Devices coupled to tubs such as Drags and to keep other devices such as blocks, dumplings and jack-catches in working order.
- To lead my pony to and from the stables and to keep a safe distance behind other ponies being led.

I HAVE BEEN WARNED

- To examine my pony and harness during the shift and report any sores, injury, loss of shoes or defective harness at once to the Deputy or Corporal and again when taking the pony back to the stables.
- To see that limbers are kept off the pony's hocks and that chains are not left hanging.
- To stand between the rails when attaching or detaching my pony.
- To uncouple pony before attempting to lift a derailed tub.

Of the penalties for not using Drags etc.

- To provide light, water and food for the pony and report a shortage.
- To report when pony catches roof or sides or any injury to pony.
- Not to leave pony coupled to tubs, but to fasten him securely to a solid support and locker up the run of tubs.
- Not to ride on the pony or tubs.
- Not to attempt to take my pony through a narrow opening.
- Not to attempt to turn my pony round between tubs or in a narrow roadway as the pony may knock out roof supports or bolt and cause injuries to me or himself.
- To report immediately any damage to the track or safety devices to my Corporal or Deputy.

(Facsimile of a form given to Bevin Boys allocated pony work at a Doncaster colliery)

Name: Colin Massingham
Born: 29 January 1925
Wartime location: Darfield, Barnsley

"I was fourteen years and three months old, starting work on the Dearne Valley screens on 1 May 1939. What a job it was. Steel-moving plates, clanking and banging about, coal flying all over ... and the job was to pick all the muck out ... stone and brass and stuff. For six days – 6.00 am to 2.00 pm – my first week's wage was 18s and 11d. We had a twenty-minute break ... snap time ... I took a bottle of tea and stood it by the side of the old steam engine that drove the screens to keep the tea hot, despite all the grease. I stuck it for two or three weeks and saw the pit-top foreman telling him I couldn't stand it much longer ... the noise was driving me dizzy. He had a job for me ... making pills for the shot-firers. I then asked to go underground.

When I started on the machines in 1940 it was a shilling or 1s 1d per ton. The tubs held half a ton, so two had to be filled ... that was for machine coal but for hand coal ... using pick, hammer and wedge ... I think that was 2s 2d a ton.

I had a short spell at Darfield Main in 1944 for three weeks. I'd heard the pay was 13s 10d a shift compared with 13s 6d at Dearne Valley. I was set on pony driving. I felt a bit timid at first going down the cage. It was OK when it was all ripped and you could stand up and walk along, but down at the face it was a shock ... top side was two foot six inch and low side just one foot nine. Men worked laid down on their sides with short-handed shovels. It was a heck of a job ... not for me.

Roof falls were regular but we always got a warning ... you'd hear a creaking, whining noise. One night shift ... there was an almighty bang and all the rock came in ... hundreds of tons ... to within ten or fifteen yards of us ... it was like a solid wall of rock, impossible to get through to save anything.

I got buried partly in 1942 and injured my shoulder and hip ... a big lump of coal came on top of me ... it caught me on the shoulder and pushed me onto the machine which had a row of jagged teeth ... it must have weighed three or four tons and held me down on the machine which was still running. My mate jumped up and switched it off. I told the deputy I was going out of the pit and asked for a note but he said he dare not give me a note even though I showed him my injuries ... there was blood running down my side but he made me stop until the end of the shift! The medical centre was just one bloke and there were no baths at the pit so I went home in my pit clothes, got bathed so I could see the damage and went to the doctor's next morning and was off work for two weeks.

The canteen was opened in July 1942. Our first dinner was free meat and potato pie. Previously, there was a small corrugated iron hut at the end of the lamp room but all that was sold were pork pies and little bottles of milk. There was no seating. We just sat down outside, on the floor. I then had to walk almost two miles to get home and bathe. Pit baths came to Dearne Valley on 17 November 1951; most of us made use of them. ”

(From *Yorkshire Mining Veterans*, Brian Elliott, Wharncliffe Publishing, 2005)

Name: Joe Hartley
Born: 21 September 1925
Wartime location: Wath-on-Dearne, Rotherham

At fourteen years of age, Joe Hartley found work constructing air raid shelters for a local builder, moving on to become a screen operative at Manvers Main colliery. He volunteered for the armed forces but declined enlistment in the submarine service, taking work as a driver with Yorkshire Farmers. Presenting himself at the recruitment centre for a second time, he got more than he bargained for and was ordered to report to Askern Main pit.

“I was shocked when I found out I was a Bevin Boy. There were lads from all over the country. I think we were the third lot to train there for a four-week spell. We spent a week underground . . . we also did physical training and ran around the countryside marching and wearing pit boots. I remember the Bevin Boys' Anthem, which went something like this:

We had to join up
We had to join up
We had to join up old Bevin's army
Fifty bob a week
Wife and kids to keep
Hob – nailed boots and blisters on your feet
We had to join up
We had to join up
We had to join old Bevin's army
If it wasn't for war
We'd be where we were before
Old Bevin you're barmy!

I was then sent to Darfield Main. I was seventeen and a half years old. I worked at the pit bottom to begin with dealing with full and empty tubs and helped with the haulage. It was very cold in the intake shaft. I wore an old boiler suit I used in my lorry driving days. One lad wore a butcher's smock. He would feed the ponies with pickled onions from his pocket. There were no pit-head baths so I came home in my muck. When you travelled on the service bus, you got some looks; passengers wanted to keep well away from you.

After about eleven months at Darfield, I got transferred back to Manvers, working underground. After a few months, I was on the face filling, using a shovel and a pick. Once, I got buried with coal on the morning shift. They pulled me out and I continued to work.”

(From *Yorkshire Mining Veterans*, Brian Elliott, Wharncliffe Books, 2005)

Name: Dennis Winterton
Born: 6 May 1918
Wartime location: Pilley, Barnsley

“I came out of the RAF on medical grounds and got a job as a blacksmith shoeing pit ponies at the Wharncliffe Silkstone Colliery, near Tankersley. I worked in the surface forge and down the pit cold shoeing. At weekends, to earn extra money, I did repair and maintenance work on cages and mechanical gear. After studying for my exams, in 1943 I became a Deputy. It was a very responsible job that was sometimes upsetting. One day, I was called to a shaft after an accident. One man was reported to be badly injured. I investigated and found that thirty tubs had run away down an incline. One miner managed to jump clear but the other was pinned under a tub and was badly injured. When I found him, to my horror, it turned out to be my wife's half brother Colin Gardner. One of his legs was almost severed and hanging on by its skin. I crawled underneath the tub on my stomach and managed to apply a tourniquet to stop the bleeding. I also gave him a shot of morphine and told the lads to carefully drag the tubs clear one by one as I got some rope and fastened up his good leg. Then we stretchered him topside and got him to hospital. His leg was amputated but he survived. It was one hell of a shock. There was mention of a bravery award at the time but nothing ever came of it.

I lived with my wife Edith in a colliery owned terraced house. Edith worked for the NAAFI on shift work providing meals for us miners.

I was always a very good singer and I sang at miners' fuddles. We used to have a singsong in Worsborough Park in the open air. I did all the standard Howard Keel parts there and in other places. I was once on BBC's *Gerry Wilmot Radio Show* and I appeared as an extra in a wartime film *We'll Meet Again*. I won lots of talent contests and I still sing for my supper today.”

Name: Irvine (Murph) Wilcock
Born: 5 July 1924
Wartime location: Daw Lane, Painthorpe, Wakefield

“Including granddad, who lived with us, there were ten members of our family. Like dad, Dennis, Eddie, Ernest, Leslie and me were all miners. In 1938, at fourteen years of age, I left school on the Friday and started work on Crigglestone pit top screens the following Monday. I worked there until I was seventeen.

During the war, I reckon we were the best-fed family in Europe. Mum was a great cook. At the weekend, breakfast was usually bacon, sausage, fried cheese and Staffordshire oak cakes made with flour and yeast. Mum was a Staffordshire girl. She could make something out of nothing and worked wonders with sheep's heads and beef hearts. And she made all our own bread – sixteen loaves at a time to last us all week.

During the week, dad would get us all up at 5.20 am sharp. He would have beef dripping and toast waiting for us every morning and all our pit clothes would be laid out ready for us in front of a roaring fire. It was only a five-minute walk to the pit. We started at 6.00 am. My job was to pick dross out of the coal, removing it from the conveyor by hand into baskets. Four baskets made a hundredweight and we got paid one-penny farthing per hundredweight. There were eight to ten lads either side of the belt. The lads at the top of the belt could obviously pick off more dross than the lads at the bottom so we rotated, taking it in turns to occupy the places at the front of the line. It was fair. I made some good wages, up to one shilling and ten pence per day. It was all quite good-natured, but one day I had a scrap with a lad called Harry. I was sent to the manager's office. He gave me two choices. Either I could volunteer to go underground or I could be sacked. I was quite keen to go below anyway, so I went back and told Harry I was leaving the screens. He was a bit put out and explained to the manager that he was equally responsible for the fight. That's how we went underground together and became lifelong best pals until Harry died in 2003.

The first job we got underground was twisting tubs, making sure that full tubs and empties were on the right rails. On 29 July 1941 there was an explosion in the pit that killed twenty-two men. My father had a lucky escape. He was due to work that day but there was some disagreement about over-manning and he wasn't needed. He was sent home. My mother's cousin was killed and the three Fox brothers from Middlestown all died that day.

After that, I went on to pony driving and I really enjoyed it. I've written a rather sad poem about working with my favourite pony. The poem's called *Stable Mates*:

A lonely old man with a wistful face gazed across the fields by the pit,
As every day on his morning stroll, on the wall by the stream he would sit.
Old Bill had retired the previous year and now he'd nothing to do,
He'd stroll round the village, his dog at his heel, just to pass an hour or two.

He saw some old ponies out of the pit; they'd been brought to the fields for a rest,
And his mind wandered back to the days of his youth and a horse that was one of the best.
All the men called him Tiny though heaven knows why, for his heart was as big as a drum,
And Bill loved him dearly; he even gave him his snap, right down to the very last crumb.

He could pull any load no matter how big, his limbs straining hard at the traces,
Hauling supplies such as girders and rails and timber to prop up the faces.
They made a good team old Tiny and Bill and, when work was finished each day,
Bill would feed Tiny a handful of oats whilst he stowed all the harness away.

Then off they would go, down the travelling road to the stables where Billy would see,
That Tiny was brushed down, watered and fed, before he went home for his tea.
T'was the same every day, week in and week out, until tragedy struck them one day,
There was a rumble like thunder and the air filled with dust and the roof started falling away.

The roof timbers shattered and crashed to the floor just where Bill and his pony were stood,
Then the rescue men came prepared for the worst and to give all the help that they could.
They dug Bill out as he lay, with this arms locked together round Tim's head.
He was terribly injured but he could not believe that the pony he worshipped was dead.

Poor Bill went to pieces when they told him the news and he wept 'till he passed out with pain,
Then they carried him out to a hospital bed where his poor broken body was lain.
Many weeks he lay there until he was fit, to work down the pit once again,
But his eyes misted over whenever he passed the spot where old Tiny was slain.

Old Bill still recalls that day in his life as he strolls through the field on the hill,
For he knows that those ponies won't return to the pits . . . and he hopes that no more ever will.

I liked the miners life but I always fancied going in the forces. I'd been to grammar school so I reckoned I might get accepted for the RAF as a bomb aimer/navigator. I volunteered and went down to Doncaster for an interview. And I passed. I was over the moon. But then came the medical and they found I was colour blind.

Feeling a bit put out, I ran away from home with the idea of joining the navy in Liverpool. I left Wakefield by train and found myself going in completely the wrong direction, finishing up in Sheffield during an air raid. I ended up sleeping in a bombed out tram and on the following day I went to Liverpool. Obviously, the word had got out and I was picked up by the police. I was interrogated, searched and stripped and my clothes were sent away to be fumigated. I spent the night in some sort of mental institution. The following day, they put me on a train for Wakefield. When I got home, mother sarcastically announced: 'Here comes the prodigal.' Dad was more understanding and forgiving. He took me on one side and said: 'Take no notice of her lad; here's ten bob. Go out and get yourself a few pints.' So I stayed in mining and looking back, those days were the happiest of my life. We were all in the same boat. We were comrades. Nothing ever got us down.

I have to admit though that I was always a bit of a bugger when I was young. I was a tearaway at work and I was sometimes a bit of a handful at home as well. In those days, women had their babies at home. Well, mum had just given birth and was resting upstairs with the baby, a neighbour called Mary helping out with the nappies and such. I was downstairs messing about with the fire, drawing it with a newspaper. I can't have been concentrating 'cause the flames set fire to the tassels on the mantelpiece runner. I managed to put the thing out but Mary told mum what had happened and she yelled out: 'Get the dog lead!' With that I was marched upstairs and told off. The dog collar was put around my neck and the lead end was tied to the bedstead and there I remained until dad got home. He laughed his head off. ”

Name: Dennis Wilcock
Born: 31 October 1929
Wartime location: Daw Lane, Painthorpe, Wakefield

“I followed my elder brother Irvin into Crigglestone Colliery pit in 1943. Like him, I was fourteen years old. My first job involved sweeping up and mashing tea but I was always keen to learn and I was very interested in watching the mechanics. So, when I was fifteen, I volunteered to work below ground as an apprentice fitter. I was taken under the wing of a marvellous man called Jack Stokes who taught me everything about the job and a hell of a lot about life as well. On that very first day underground, I was taken to the face where those twenty-two miners had been killed in the 1941 explosion. There were twenty-two white crosses to mark the spots where each body had been found. That awful sight really brought home to me the dangers of mining.

Like Irvin, I had an early inclination to enlist in the navy but at the age of seventeen you had to have both parents signatures on the application form. Mum would have signed but dad insisted that I'd started my apprenticeship so I should stick with mining. I served my apprenticeship until I was twenty-one, then I became responsible for all the mechanical services on the night shift.

Later I enrolled in Crigglestone's underground fire fighting team and I served my country by joining the Auxiliary Fire Service in Wakefield for six years. I was the captain of Crigglestone Fire Team at the time. We once got to the divisional finals, which were held on Doncaster Racecourse. It consisted of running out hosepipes on a mock coalface and I did the main run in 21.8 seconds and we won the finals – a record time. The competition was then disbanded. So I can say to my grandchildren that every time we pass Doncaster Racecourse granddad holds a record time on that course that will never be broken.

As the war progressed, we were asked to work even harder to boost output and we agreed to work Saturdays. We consistently broke production targets, my father and all my brothers playing their part, not forgetting my mother who worked tirelessly for the British Legion. Father eventually died of pneumoconiosis – you only had damp rags to put over your mouths in those days – but remarkably me an Irvine are still going strong. ”

. . . NAAFI ASSISTANTS

The Navy, Army, Air Force Institute (NAAFI) was set up as an official canteen and refreshment organisation aimed at providing serving off-duty men and women with home-like dining and relaxation facilities. NAAFI workers wore no uniform and were not subject to military rules or discipline, Typically, they worked as food preparation and kitchen assistants and cooks, the pay rates varying from £1 per week for counter assistants to £2 5s for qualified cooks. Some staff worked away from home and were entitled to financial help with board and lodgings.

Name: Edith Winterton
Born: 24 November 1920
Wartime location: Pilley, Barnsley

“I started work with the NAAFI in 1942, working in the pit canteen at the Wharncliffe Silkstone Colliery, near Tankersley. My husband Dennis – we were married in 1936 – was a miner so we qualified for a colliery-terraced house in Stone Row. It was built of stone with no bathroom and no heating other than a coal fire but it had a small scullery. The toilet was across the yard. We had to leave a paraffin lamp in there on cold winter nights to stop it from freezing. I did all my washing in a copper, building a fire underneath it to boil our clothes. I don't know why I bothered some times. You'd dry your washing in the pit yard but what with all the smoke and the grit, it'd be worse than when you'd hung it out.

There were eight or ten ladies working two eight hour shifts in the canteen. I had some lovely friends there. We mucked in with all the jobs. Sometimes you'd be preparing vegetables and or serving food and sometimes you'd be washing up in the deep wooden sinks. There was always plenty of food. It was plain but wholesome. We made lots of bacon sandwiches for the miners' snap. There were great trays of the stuff covered in hot water. And we did things like meat and potato pie, stews and bread and butter and rice puddings. You never stood around doing nothing. I worked in the canteen for eighteen months before I started working from home hairdressing. It's something I'd done before the war.

I cut and set ladies hair heating my curling tongs on a gas ring or on a mentholated spirit stove. I charged 1s 6d for a full wave. And I did re-sets. I had two hair dryers in my front room. Lots of miners wives came for their hair doing. After a while, I started going round to local houses offering home perms. It provided welcome spare cash for food.

I have to say, we ate pretty well. We had a family of diabetics next door who couldn't afford their bacon ration so we had this arrangement. They'd get the bacon and I'd buy it off them. I could make a meal out of a single slice of corned beef. We were happy to get that. Sometimes I'd get a piece of lamb knuckle from the butcher – all bone and fat. I'd boil it up in our coal oven and skim off the fat. That went into a chip pan to fry our chips – we couldn't afford lard in those days. We'd get some meat off it and the rest would make soup. My mother-in-law kept a few hens as well so we were never went hungry. ”

... TRAIN DRIVERS

The war machine would have ground to a halt but for the vital role played by the nation's railways, raw materials, munitions, armaments, factory goods, fuel, foodstuffs, military personnel and commuting workers and other passengers all needing a reliable service. The strategic importance of the railways was recognised by the enemy, railway lines, shunting yards and stations becoming major targets in air raids. Freight trains were a favourite opportunistic target for marauding Luftwaffe pilots. At night, conventional running lights were extinguished but, especially in moonlight, enemy pilots looked out for tell tale smoke and sparks and the giveaway glows from fireboxes. Under blackout conditions, the job of driving steam engines at night was particularly hazardous. At the outbreak of war, passengers had to cope at night with a complete blackout but by December 1939 dim boxed-lighting had been installed in carriages to counter the problems. The four major rail companies were taken under government control for the duration of hostilities, the fledgling British Railways actually returning a profit. Some trains were so packed and chaotic that some of the more agile passengers had to enter and exit through windows.

On 28/29 April 1941, York Station came under sustained attack from the air, a 250-pound bomb narrowly missing the newly arrived express from London. A shower of incendiaries left six passenger carriages and the station roof burning, another high explosive bomb falling on the roundhouse where all twenty locomotives parked around the central turntable were damaged. The crack, streamlined Pacific class engine *Sir Ralph Wedgewood* laid twisted on its side.

Name: Walter Salmon
Born: 22 June 1902
Wartime location: Hull
(Memories recalled by his daughter Hilary B. Blackburne)

❝Father left Grimsby in the 1920s and came to Hull to work for the London and North Eastern Railway Company [LNER], first as a cleaner, then a fireman and later as a driver. During the war he was located at the LNER's Springhead (Anlaby) Depot and I remember him being selected to be part of a small group of drivers who received special instruction on how to remove vital parts from engines so that they could not be driven by the enemy in the event of an invasion. For that reason, he was exempt from military service. Dad did his bit by driving trains carrying both troops and ammunition and was very proud of the fact that he drove the first trainload of child evacuees out of Hull. Once he had a very lucky escape when he brought his engine and a whole load of wagons over an unexploded bomb, which, happily unbeknown to him at the time, had buried itself in the permanent way between the lines. Father didn't come out of the war completely unscathed. Once he missed his footing in the blackout, falling from the footplate of his locomotive onto the rails and bruising several ribs. Sometime later, the blackout was responsible for a crash just outside Hessle station when his train was in collision with a fish train. This time he suffered severe shock which resulted in a series of heart attacks. ”

... PORTER-GUARDS

Assisting civilian passengers and troops to their seats, closing doors, and blowing departure whistles. These were the more mundane and traditional duties of porter-guards, augmented in wartime by additional responsibilities such as blackout regulations enforcement and, in the absence of station nameplates, advising passengers when to alight.

On the night of the raid in York, porters in the railway station performed the vital task of kicking incendiary bombs off the platforms and onto the tracks:

“Trains were slow and uncertain and wayward, lit by blue-painted lamps that cast a faint and ghastly glow on the travellers, reducing them to anonymity. The trains might be taking you home, to new and unexpected perspectives, to holes in the road and gaps in the terraces, or they might be taking you back. Their common purpose, it seemed, was to prove how many people could be crammed into one coach. Here no holds were barred. Authority was held in a kind of affectionate derision. Luggage racks served as hammocks. The hardy ones squatted on the floor, amid the boots and the cigarette ends and the kitbags. The disinherited stood in the freezing corridors and sometimes stared with envy and sheer hatred at those jammed in the compartments. One of your neighbours might be a dazed and inarticulate Polish airman wondering what on earth the English had to grin about; another a Free French soldier inquiring where he might find the opportunity to play 'le table tennis' in such a beleaguered island. Wherever you were installed, you stayed there until you reached your journey's end. And whenever you could, you slept, waking as often as not to find a total stranger resting his head on your shoulder. And of course, you didn't care. For this was the sleep of comrades.”

(Recollections of John Fearnley published in the *Sheffield Star*, 'Sheffield Blitz' Anniversary Edition, November 1965.)

Five hundred and fifty-one employees of the London North Eastern Railway were killed in the Second World War. A memorial designed by Sir Edward Lutyens was erected in Station Road, York to commemorate their sacrifice.

Name: Peggy Callaghan
Born; 22 October 1921
Wartime location: Wellington Lane, off Beverley Road, Hull

“I was employed by the London, North Eastern Railway (LNER) and went out daily in the local trains and was involved in two separate 'secret movements'. I lived opposite the railway offices. My dad who was a firewatcher for the premises was friendly with the railway firewatcher and he took him into the railway offices to show him the passages below in the basement. These led to a secret movement room to which despatch riders came and went with orders for troops and ammo' train movements.

One late shift I was told by the station inspector to take the set on platform six out. When I asked 'where to?' he said something like ' 'tell you later.'

I cannot remember whether I was ever told my destination. However, when I arrived on platform six I found a set consisting of ten (through corridor) coaches being shunted – and it was already occupied – completely full of German POW's! Their army escort told me they had come straight from the front and they certainly looked like it. The smell was quite strong and they were the enemy but I can remember feeling sorry and embarrassed for them.

We set off and I know it was the Hull-Scarborough line. We didn't have any stops and everything was blacked out – stations names etc. I cannot say for sure where we finally stopped, only that it was somewhere past Bridlington. There were army personnel on the platform to help get the POW's onto trucks outside the blacked out station. After the train had emptied, I went right through the set with the sergeant from Paragon Station looking into toilets and under seats etc to make sure everyone had got off!

Another time, I was on the same line with the same amount of carriages but this time it was our own Red Berets going, I think into some special training and I had an idea it was Carnaby where they got off. This used to be an airfield and when the Arnhem Bridge affair happened later, I wondered if some of the paratroopers involved were the boys who had been dropped off 'somewhere along the East Coast' by yours truly and our engine driver and fireman of course? ”

... FISHERMEN

At the outbreak of war, the British fishing fleet comprised 1030 steam trawlers. Of these, 816 were requisitioned for military use, mainly as minesweepers, convoy escorts and anti-submarine vessels, crewed by former fishermen who were conscripted into the Royal Navy Reserve. The remaining 214 trawlers were manned by old men and boys not required for military service. The older, less efficient and in some cases unseaworthy boats left in the fleet, caught fewer fish and were more vulnerable to bad weather and enemy action than the newer vessels. A total of thirty-nine trawlers were lost to what were euphemistically recorded as 'marine causes'. An additional thirteen were sunk by German gunfire from submarines, twenty-three sank as a result of air attack, twenty-five fell victim to mines and twenty-four were lost to unknown causes. There were 827 fatalities including eighty-eight skippers, fishermen's bravery being acknowledged in the award of thirty-four MBE's and thirty-six BEMs. The price of fish was extremely high.

The impoverished fleet caught less than one quarter of the pre-war tonnage, Hull, Britain's most modern port, loosing, at the outbreak of war, all but two of its trawlers and its pre-eminence as a fishing station. In 1938, 287,310 tons of fish were landed in Hull. By 1941, this figure had dropped dramatically to 2,607 tons. Fishing continued from Yorkshire's minor centres like Scarborough, Whitby and Staithes, some of the shortfall in landings being made up by the bulk importation of Iceland fish into Hull on board fish carriers. The largest consignment was one of 996 tons brought by *Finlande*. By 1943, the old Hull trawlers *Bempton*, *Cave*, *Dandara*, *Filey*, *John Gilman*. *Limeslade* and the more modern *Lincolnshire,* were replaced by more modern vessels and were released by the Admiralty to resume fishing. With bunkers crammed for five-week voyages, the trawlers would assemble at the mouth of the Humber and would join northbound convoys to Aberdeen. From there, they would proceed unprotected to the Icelandic fishing grounds.

Amazingly, fish was never rationed during the war although it became a scarce treat, its price increasing seventeen-fold by 1941. Strange varieties began to appear on fishmongers' slabs, the public having to find new recipes for odd-looking creatures like ling, dogfish and catfish. And then there was the ubiquitous whale meat ('but it's not fish!') and the much-recommended salt cod that tasted like boiled socks. The Ministry of Food was again prominent in recommending experimentation:

> When fisher-folk are brave enough
> To face mines and foe for you
> You surely can be bold enough
> To try fish of a kind that's new.

Fried fish and chips was an iconic, particularly northern dish that had almost mystical properties every bit as nourishing as fabled ambrosia, that blessed trinity – the continuing availability of fresh fish, home grown potatoes and coal to fire the solid fuel frying ranges – sustaining hearts and minds. But there was another less obvious benefit from maintaining catches. During the war, regardless of rationing, air raids and other hardships, Britain's war babies were the healthiest the nation has ever produced. This astonishing reality was in no small measure due to the availability of freely dispensed cod liver oil, in 1939, Hull and Grimsby trawler owners leading the nutritional way in establishing a cooperative that eventually became known as British Cod Liver Oils Ltd.

In 1940, the crews of Scarborough trawlers, drifters and open cobbles were regularly attacked by enemy aircraft, the first incident taking place on 12 January when the *Persian Empire* and the *Riby* were subjected to bombing and machine gun fire, the *Riby*'s compass, dynamo and wireless sustaining blast damage. On 3 April the drifter *Silver Line* intervened in a dogfight between an RAF Spitfire and a Heinkel bomber. Already damaged in the exchange, the bomber was hit by ten bullets from the drifter's Lewis gun and brought down, skipper Watkinson and his men rescuing the German crew and delivering them at gunpoint to port. On 16 October 1940, three fishermen, William Colling, Francis Crawford and John Robinson were killed as their vessel, the *Pride*, hit a mine in the harbour mouth.

In a supreme epitome of the utter ruthlessness and wastefulness of war, on 27 April 1941, the fully loaded 943-ton fish carrier SS *Celte* was sunk en route from Reykjavik to Hull by Focke Wulf Condor aircraft off the Faeroe Islands.

Name: Walter (Dillinger) Denton
Born: 8 September 1916
Wartime location: Hessle Road, Hull

Robin Hood, Dick Turpin ... and Walter Denton. Someday, someone will write a novel about Hull's larger than life trawlerman that will ignite the already considerable legend and elevate his name to Yorkshire's hall of fame. But his story, a swashbuckling tale that epitomises the life-on-the-edge, devil-may-care, rip-roaring drinks-all-round attitude of fisherman the world over, unlike those of our other famous villains, needs no exaggerating. Remarkably, every word is true.

Cheeky, prank loving Walter joined Hull's trawling fleet as a trainee deck-hand, his bold, hot-headed and often dangerous antics soon earning him the nickname 'Dillinger' after United States Public Enemy No. 1 – John Dillinger whose bank robberies and confrontations with the cops brought world wide notoriety. There are two explanations as to the root of the name, the most commonly accepted version alluding to an ice chopping session with fellow deckhands. After one hand called Denton a 'lazy bastard', he grabbed a mallet in temper and clubbed him to the deck, an amazed onlooker crying out: 'Who the hell do you think you are? You're worse than John Dillinger'. Another alternative suggests that the name arises after Walter smuggled aboard a number of November 5th firecrackers. These were ignited at the moment a startled mate began to unload a heaving cod end, the furious mate screaming: 'You're worse than Dillinger!'

Like the gangster, Walter Denton, earned respect amongst the working community. He grafted hard and spent freely when ashore, always looking to spice up the day with some tomfoolery. On one occasion, he rode into a Hull pub on a horse. One another, he entered the same pub struggling with a thick mooring rope on the threshold. Cursing in a tug-of-war with a recalcitrant beast outside, he shouted: 'Come on you bastard!' and promptly dragged in a tiny puppy. Denton and his mates spent long hours swearing and carousing in the pub, a gracious routine accompanying his familiar order for beer. When his round was called, he would roll up a pound note in his palms and toss it to the barman with the words: 'Get some more slurp over here.' Unfazed by position or authority, he was a thorn in the side of many a skipper, on several voyages fooling them with feigned injury into broaching liquor stores. Once, he was taken up to the wheelhouse clutching his fist and screaming as a two-ton otter-board crashed against the side of the boat, the skipper only realising the hoax after Denton had taken several swigs of whisky. A similar ruse worked on a second terrified skipper, the wag surreptitiously placing a beating coley heart in his mouth and ejecting its blood to fake a haemorrhage. But Denton's most famous adventure took place on dry land, lightening the gloom of even World War Two.

Kicking his heels one day between voyages, Dillinger found himself idly watching the scene outside Bevin House on George Street in Hull, dozens of young mothers queuing inside to collect their allocations of National Dried Milk coupons for their babies who were parked in their prams on the pavement. Game for a laugh, Dillinger and his accomplice Pat Petrini took pity on a coloured baby languishing in a rather battered old pram and promptly decided to remove him to a more regal looking vehicle. The two babies were swapped around and then two more until the entire fleet of perambulators had new occupants. What a hoot! But on their return, the perplexed mothers were not amused and called the police, order and babies being restored as the two rogues left for the pub.

Generous to a fault, helpful to old ladies and those worse off than himself, Denton, like other trawlermen of his ilk, would spend all his earnings on boozy 'dingdongs'. He would dress flashily and travel by taxi and if he had any money left before his next voyage, it was tossed, as was the custom, on the pavement as a treat for street urchins.

Denton was a fearless jackanapes in peace and an equally courageous volunteer in war, joining dangerous missions to collect vital ball bearings from manufacturers in Sweden. Enlisting in crews chosen for their 'venturous spirit and reliability' he sailed on fast motor gun boats on the 1,000 mile round trips from Hull to Lysekil near Gothenburg, completing several missions mainly during the winter of 1943–44. Later, he helped crew converted trawlers and he had to abandon ship twice. While awaiting rescue in a lifeboat after one enemy attack, he heard a fellow shipmate lamenting the loss of a gold wedding ring left aboard in a locker. Without more ado, he plunged over the side and swam to the stricken vessel before she sank, rescuing the ring. Its owner was flabbergasted and overwhelmed, Dillinger nonchalantly pointing to a bottle of retrieved rum that was, he explained, the real object of his swim.

. . . SCHOOLBOYS and SCHOOLGIRLS

War was declared as the autumn school term was about to commence, the fear of immediate bombing causing widespread classroom closures while air raid shelters were built. A home tuition scheme was introduced, teachers providing lessons in English, maths and contemporary studies in private houses away from bomb vulnerable areas. Some establishments like Queen Margaret's School in Scarborough – it was displaced by the needs of service personnel, the children finding themselves in the opulent surroundings of Castle Howard in Ryedale – were relocated for the duration. Other students also found themselves on the move, 160 of the senior boys of Hymers College in Hull finding alternative accommodation within the ancient precincts of the private school in Pocklington. When the majority of schools re-opened, children practiced air raid precautions as a sort of game, learning evacuation techniques and how to use gas masks. Each child was issued with an emergency pack consisting of Horlicks tablets, earplugs and chewing gum, the gum to be placed between the teeth to stop tongue biting during air raids. At lunchtime, children tucked into the British staple – National Loaf sandwiches made from dry and coarse bread packed with ubiquitous corned beef or a little cheese. Many children had to walk or cycle to and from school often over great distances, as public transport was very limited and infrequent.

In rural establishments like Pocklington School, students were encouraged to help farmers in between lessons. They were also asked to fill sandbags for the local authority and assist in the cultivation of the school's vegetable plot. That particular school was adjacent to a newly developed RAF airfield and when the first Wellington bomber touched down in 1941, the excitement disrupted a game of cricket, players and spectators leaving the field to watch the landing. The commissioning of new runways, however, led to an attack by the Luftwaffe on 21 September 1941, a stick of anti-personnel bombs intended for the airbase straddling the school buildings and causing £900 worth of damage but no fatalities. One stray bomb fragment flew horizontally along the length of a long dormitory, crazing a mirror over the head prefect's bed.

The war severely disrupted education and the normal routines of childhood but it also provided unprecedented adventures and freedom, the natural daredevil inclinations of young boys having full rein, For a decade, cowboy and Indian fantasies gave way to nearer-to-home make-believe, schoolboys with wooden guns pretending to be soldiers and RAF pilots, aircraft spotting becoming a popular pastime, the 6d Penguin *Observers Guide to Aircraft Silhouettes* achieving outstanding sales. Boys became avid souvenir hunters collecting scraps of parachute fabric, wrecked aircraft parts, shrapnel and even live ordnance, on several occasions taking unexploded devices into the classroom.

With fathers and mothers totally committed to the war effort, chores were the bane of youngsters' lives and at all ages they were expected to contribute to domestic life, vegetable gardening, the gathering of fuel and wild fruit from the hedgerows and the collection of recyclable materials that could be useful to the war effort occupying much of their time. And when they were old enough to pull a trigger, they couldn't wait to join up.

Name: John Roger Frost
Born: 25 July 1924
Wartime location: St Peter's School, Bootham, York

"I was bought up in Hornsea where I went to preparatory school with the actor Brian Rix. After my father left, I went to St Peter's with my mother in 1938. Mother went as a house matron. She was determined I should have a good education. Being good at sport, especially cricket – I was mad on cricket – I got a part scholarship. Mother was a remarkable woman. Three years later, she became the headmaster's secretary and taught herself shorthand and typing.

My first big memory was the evacuation of Dunkirk. We were all terrified. France had capitulated and we all thought that that was the end. We expected the Germans to land on the coast at any minute.

The war affected academic life at St Peter's quite a lot. The bulk of the teachers were called up or volunteered. They got all sorts of staff in but many were not of the same quality. Of course, many of the older chaps remained. The school was all male in those days and we were always hungry. Food was a big problem. We always got something filling – shepherds pie and masses of potatoes and plum duff pudding in the middle of the day. That was the main meal. Each house had its own facilities. At teatime we were given tea and sandwiches – no dinner -and then two hours of prep before we were rushed off to bed at eight o'clock. I was fourteen years old. Every boy had masses of watery cocoa before bedtime. We all moved our stomachs and you could hear it sloshing about. In summer, it was still light but we slept like tops, as we were so tired. We were ready for it having been on the go from seven o'clock. They really worked us hard. We didn't have a spare minute.

I remember the fagging. Fags could be called upon to work for older boys for a whole year. I was a fag. Some of the monitors took huge delight at beating a fag. The masters used to cane us on the backside with a stick but the monitors were only allowed to use a slipper. But they always inflicted the maximum pain by using the heel end. They could give you a maximum of six strokes. You had the right of appeal to a housemaster but nobody ever wanted to be thought of as a squealer.

Most of us joined the School Cadet Force. We were given uniforms and were put in charge of an ex-Army Sergeant Major by the name of Puttick. He issued us with Lee-Enfield rifles and bayonets. Once or twice a week we'd parade, practicing drill and presenting arms. I felt rather grown up at the time realising that most of the Home Guards like my uncle were parading with pitchforks and scythes. We were taught to shoot – we used .22 ammunition on the school's rifle range – using adapted rifles. We were shown how to clean our weapons and 'pull through' drawing a length of greased material down the barrel. Being a good shot, I was soon recruited to the school's shooting team. It got rather more serious when we were allowed to fire regulation ammunition on a proper army range at Strensall. The cracks nearly deafened you.

The school had a band, my house supplying the drums and cymbals. I was landed with the wretched cymbals! I hadn't the faintest idea about tunes or music and I used to clang them at the wrong minute.

Once a year we were sent out to work on a farm at Coulton near Hovingham. The headmaster had a cottage and a bit of land there. We helped with the haymaking and the milking. They worked us very hard. My mother and my sister helped run the campsite and they did the cooking for us.

'Entertainment? What's that? We had radios in our dormitories and listened to them. We were all fascinated. All we wanted to do was to leave school and join the forces. There was a cinema opposite the school. Once or twice a term, we were allowed to go see a picture. And sometimes we'd sneak out to the *Old Grey Mare* pub at Clifton and have a shandy. The landlord turned a blind eye. On one occasion they took the entire school down to York railway station for an engine naming ceremony. All the big wigs from the railway company were there – I think it must have been 1940 or 1941 – to see the naming of St Peter's School, York.

In the last year at school, I enrolled in the Home Guard. Once a week we had to do a night duty, looking out for incendiaries or parachutists. There were eight of us doing two-hour shifts. We wore our uniforms and we carried rifles in case we saw any Germans. My house was bombed in the Baedeker Raid of 1942*. The school term hadn't started but I'd returned early. When the sirens sounded we retreated to the cellars with the maids. There were multiple explosions and bangs and crashes and the school was badly damaged. All the women were panicking and screaming. When the raid was over, the housemaster – a wonderful man called Kenneth Rhodes – he was devoted to the school – came out and saw that the roof was on fire. He immediately jumped on an old bicycle and went into York to see if he could find a fire engine. I could see that my own house was on fire but something else worried me more than that. One high explosive bomb had dropped on the playing fields, showering earth and stones all over my precious cricket field! ”

* 28/29 April 1942.

Name: Brian Dunning
Born: 1932
Wartime location: Lawnswood, Leeds and London

“At the time of Dunkirk, I was living in Leeds, being eight or nine years old. For some obscure reason, hundreds of soldiers, weary and in battledress appeared on a strip of grass near our house in Otley Old Road, Lawnswood. Most of them were lying down asleep. Mrs Brown, the next-door neighbour, took one of the soldiers in. He stayed for a couple of nights and gave me an army penknife. It was a bit rusty so I solemnly told my pals that it was Dunkirk rust. I didn't really know where Dunkirk was – but I had a vague idea that something had happened there to explain the presence of so many soldiers in Lawnswood – of all places.

In 1941, my father Alfred, then a Leeds school teacher, took a job with the BBC in London and the family found itself in a small hotel at the entrance to Bushey Park, Hampton Court. The park was (I think) not yet the HQ of SHAEF (Supreme Headquarters Allied Expeditionary Force) and indeed the United States was still neutral. But within a year to eighteen months, it was Ike's planning base. He lived nearby at Kingston-on-Thames. By then, we'd moved into a house at East Molesey, just across the Thames from Hampton Court. I attended school at Kingston Grammar and to get there I had to scamper across Hampton Court Bridge to catch the trolley bus. One morning, a SHAEF car stopped. The front door swung open and I got in. Ten minutes later, I arrived at school and got out. No conversation. No handshakes. Boys of ten just accept life as it comes and don't ask questions. But I'm pretty certain that the female driver was Kay Summersby and I'm also pretty certain that the officer in the back seat (I sat up front) was Eisenhower himself. He and Kay are alleged to have had a relationship. I think there were a couple more lifts.

Incidentally, when the bombing got uncomfortable, we retreated one summer to Fylingdales near Whitby (where we spent our pre-war holidays), leaving poor old Dad in London. I can still see the huge convoys sailing north off the Yorkshire coast and can only presume they were gathering for the Murmansk run. ”

SHAEF was formed in December 1943 and charged with planning Operation Overlord – the invasion of France. The majority of the operational staff were accommodated in specially erected buildings within the park. Kay Summersby was the Major General's chauffeuse, later becoming his personal secretary and military aide. In her book recalling memories of the war years – *Eisenhower Was My Boss* – Summersby makes no reference to any clandestine affair, although in her 1976 autobiography she suggests that her relationship with Ike was common knowledge on both sides of the Atlantic.

Name: Ernest Smith
Born: 1930
Wartime location: Sand Hill Farm, Holme-on-Spalding Moor

“I was ten years old when war broke out. I lived with my parents on a farm, which has been in the family since 1871. My son farms it now. Other farms have amalgamated but our farm is still as it was.

I used to go to school in the village, crossing the bomber airfield every day. But I didn't like school. If there'd been an air raid – the airfield was targeted a few times – school didn't used to start until 10.30. The teachers and our headmaster were in the ARP and if they'd been up all night, they slept in the next day. I liked that.

We were glad as well if the sirens started after dinner time because we could leave school early and it was usually not worth going back. We had to stay with friends just down the road, but we liked it there. Some school days, dad asked me to work on the farm. I enjoyed it better than going to school. The following day when the headmaster asked me where I'd been, I told him I was needed on the farm. Everyone wanted food so there were no further questions asked.

There were constant flights from the airfield. There were lots of Canadians there. One day, there was an awful crash as a plane attempted to take off with a bomb load of incendiaries. The plane crashed into a ditch and all seven crew members – all Canadians I think – were killed. Just a few more yards and they might have made it. Crew records exist but no one ever approached us about a memorial. For years afterwards we boys would find live ammunition in the banks of that ditch.

I remember the army arriving at the farm on manoeuvres. They took our two front rooms as their HQ and stopped two or three days. The batmen slept in our kitchen and the ordinary soldiers in outbuildings and hedgerows. Sometimes they came at potato picking time and the officers volunteered the men to help with the picking.

We had two German POWs on the farm – 'German John' came first. I wondered if I could communicate with him and I said slowly and deliberately: 'It's – a – nice – day.' 'Sure is a nice day,' he replied in an American accent. It turns out that in 1932 he'd been a student working on a farm in Iowa. He'd been working in the Red Cross Ambulance Corps in Italy where he was taken prisoner. Back home in Germany, he had a forty-acre farm in Bremerhaven. He communicated very well and he helped us communicate with the other German.

Fred Heinemann came along a month later to work for us. He was from East Germany. He couldn't speak hardly any English at all but 'German John' could translate. Both men came to the farm on a daily basis on a truck from Storwood about ten miles away just west of Melbourne. They wore POW uniforms. They were both excellent workers and needed no supervision.

For a while, 'German John' thought that Hitler was improving Germany by providing such things as autobahns and was avenging his country for what happened in World War One, but he soon felt differently about it. I can honestly say that I made friends with both men. They were both kept on a long time after the war and helped clear the snow in the winter of 1947. Just before Fred left, he sent us a very heart warming and moving letter*. He went back home and we never heard from him again, but 'German John' kept in touch and he came back to see us with his grandson about twenty years ago. ”

*A photocopy of the letter is included under the heading 'Days in the Lives of Prisoners of War'.

Name: Dennis Simpson
Born: 4 November 1926
Wartime location: Milner Farm, Old Town, Micklefield
(Dennis died during the writing of this book, on 29 May 2006)

“We spent a lot of time in the hedgerows picking berries to make various drinks – elderberry wine, parsnip wine and hip syrup. Elderberry was my favourite and we used to have a cup of this warm in a morning before going to school. In wartime, I was expected to catch a rabbit regularly to supplement our meat ration. I set my snickles on my way to school and on Sunday mornings I would go with the men ferreting and digging out rabbits. I'd also gather water hen and pewit eggs for my mother and she would fry up twelve in a pan at once. Collecting horsehair, flint stones and rabbit skins for sale were all ways of earning extra money for mother's housekeeping.

At school, we were taught patriotic songs and how to use a gas mask. When we became fourteen, we were expected to join the Air Raid Patrol (ARP) and the Police Messenger Service. We were shown how to shoot a pistol and given details of all the Home Guard and ARP headquarters in the district. This was all in case of German occupation. We would have been the Underground like they had in France. We had a wonderful teacher – Sergeant Bobby Todd. He taught discipline and respect and in return our parents thought a lot of him. His discipline was based on a cuff round the lughole. I don't recall a single burglary or transgression in that village. He taught us first aid and what we should do in the event of bombing. At that time, from the age of fourteen to seventeen, I became a firewatcher on the roof of Trevellyan Chambers, a four storey building on Boar Lane in the middle of Leeds. There was a caretaker and myself with six buckets of sand and six of water. I often wonder what we could have done with these. We also had an extinguisher each. The operation lasted from 6.00 pm to 7.00 am next morning when I caught the milk train home for my breakfast. I was paid 2 shillings (10p) per week. We sometimes stood on the top of the building and watched the fire glow from the Sheffield bombing in the distance, thanking our lucky stars that they avoided Leeds.

At the time, I lived on a farm when food and sweet rationing was at its worst. The grocer would call on Thursday nights and deliver our meagre rations. Mother would have to perform miracles to eke out the small rations of margarine, bacon and other groceries. We lived on bread and potatoes. Coal was rationed and one of my chores was to find wood in the hedgerows.

There was a big shortage of staff at the time and us children were expected to work in the fields, particularly at harvest time. I drove three horses pulling a binder. We couldn't afford a leather saddle so my father used to put a Hessian sack over the horses' withers with Massey Harris Band* for stirrups. At the end of an eight-hour session, the sweat from the horse would come through the sack and the inside of my legs would be chapped with all the sweat and the friction. Father would rub me down with a dock leaf.

I'd work on the farm at other times as well. In October we'd harvest potatoes and sugar beet throughout the winter along with mangolds (mangel–wurzel). They had to be hand worked. If you used a fork, they would bleed and on a raw November morning, I can think of nothing worse than handling mangolds.

I helped kill two pigs – one in November and one in March. We sold the four legs as hams, when in fact there are only two hams on a pig. Farmers took advantage of the state of affairs by killing extra pigs and poultry in sheds out of sight of officialdom. But some of the officials were in fact, our best customers.

Sometimes I'd stand at the farmhouse door watching the bombers taking off from the airfields. I'd see them come limping back in the morning with their engines shot away and parts blown off. We had a pantry in the house with stone slabs on legs. Mother would make a bed for us under there when the air-raid sounded.”

* String used for tying up corn sheaves and bales of corn.

Name: Richard Stewart Riley
Born: 13 February 1939
Wartime location: Beckfield Lane, Acomb, York

“I was born in the Holgate Nursing Home and I lived with my parents Harry and Alice Riley along with my brother John. When war broke out dad volunteered for the army but because of his age, young family, trade skills and the fact that he'd served from 1916–18 in World War One, he was not accepted. The downside of this was that he later became directed labour.

He was well known and respected in York as a bench joiner and there were many firms who wanted to employ him but couldn't. At one point, he was directed to work in the railway carriage works making wings for gliders to be used in the Normandy landings unbeknown to the workers at the time. He worked alongside long standing railway workers who had no sense of urgency and were very wasteful of materials. He found this difficult to accept.

He was sent to work for Hills, a door manufacturing company that had taken over the Terry's chocolate factory. He used a copy lathe to make wooden propellers, later discovering that they were for obsolete aircraft and once delivered were destroyed.

Along with several others, he volunteered for the Home Guard. They would meet on the Knavesmire for various drills and dummy practice with a rocket battery. It was only fired once and that was by mistake. The rocket had not been elevated properly and it landed in the grounds of Bishopthorpe Palace. He fell out with the Home Guard as he couldn't stand being yelled at by a young officer who should have been doing army service. He said it took three men and a three-ton wagon to come and collect the officer's tin hat! He did take up Air Raid warden duties though, his duties consisting of a number of neighbours meeting up for a stroll in the evening and in dad's case, chance to have a pipe of tobacco.

By 1943, he became so frustrated with being directed to jobs that he saw as a waste of time and effort, that he became self-employed. This had its own problems as materials were severely restricted and timber permits were only issued for essential work. He started with a handcart but later managed to buy an old Ford Eight van that had been used for milk rounds. It had seen better days but at least he was mobile.

York being a non-industrial city was not subject to many air raids. There were only two of any significance. One was thought to be a mistaken target with bombers dropping their loads unable to find either Leeds or Sheffield. The other was said to be a reprisal for the terror bombing of Lübeck, a civilian target in Germany. Aircraft had followed a train into York using the light of the boiler fire on the footplate as a guide.

Other bombs were dropped from time to time as aircraft offloaded unable to find their targets. One fell on Beckfield Lane about ten or twelve doors away. Family tradition has it that it exploded at about 7.30 am. Dad would have been passing on his cycle but had forgotten his sandwiches and returned home to get them. The damage was not too extensive; the corner of the roof of one semi-detached and the bathroom of another. Poppleton Road Primary and Junior School was hit and the top floor of the centre section remained boarded up until after the war. Some property near the school was also bombed with some loss of life.

With the blackout, it was possible to see the sky lit up when there was heavy bombing of Hull docks. Air raid shelters were issued. Initially, we didn't have one but some neighbours across the road did. Theirs was an Anderson shelter; a dug out. It was partly dug into the ground then a heavy gauge parabolic shaped galvanised steel structure erected. The spoil from the digging out was thrown over the top. It smelled of damp earth. There was no heat and no lights. I have clear memories of being carried across the road one night to the sound of anti-aircraft fire to shelter in the neighbour's dug-out.

Later, we were provided with a Morrison shelter. This was a table shelter with very strong steel corner posts, a steel tabletop and some form of meshing below on which to lay a bed mattress. It was very large and dominated the dining room leaving little room for furniture. I remember using it one night when grandma came over from Leeds to stay. We had a rare treat for tea; a tin of sardines. For a reason I never understood, grandma insisted that the tin be burnt in the fire grate. I can smell it to this day with us all crammed into the shelter following an air raid warning. We could hardly wait for the all-clear. The shelter served another purpose. It made a great den for John and me to play games in.

There were a number of large brick shelters just off Lidgett Grove and several large static water tanks for use against incendiaries. The shelters made great playgrounds for local children. We would gather dried grass and light fires in them, daring each other to run through them holding our breaths against the smoke. The fit would climb up onto the large concrete flat roofs and run around. The brave would jump off. I always lowered myself more gently to the ground. My father, having a great fear of water, forbade us to go near the water tanks. Sadly, a little girl whose brother I knew did get into one and drowned.

The sirens remain a strong memory along with one other; the Halifax bomber. York was surrounded by bomber stations – Linton-on-Ouse, Elvington, Tockwith and Rufforth which was the closest, being only two to three miles from Beckfield Lane. It was not a large station but the flight path was over our house and I clearly remember the throb of engines as they laboured away on take off. In my child's eye, the Halifax was the heroic bomber before the Lancaster.

Rationing of course was a big feature of wartime, not only food of course but of coal. Our house was a typical pre-war three bedroom detached house. The kitchen was very small with a sink, built in cupboard and a gas oven. Gas was available through a meter which mostly took shillings but also single pennies. Gas was always available when you could afford it, but pressure would be very low on a Sunday when most people were cooking Sunday dinner. Sunday dinner in the Riley house was at 12.00 noon sharp. Mum would insist on having the back door open when cooking vegetables and in winter, the house would be bitterly cold.

Rationing and shortages obviously had an impact on our lifestyle but you didn't necessarily notice it all the time. Mum was very good at making the most of what there was and dad with his views on waste helped things along. To this day, my youngest daughter says nobody can get the last bit of jam out of a jar as well as I can. Dad kept hens so there were eggs and now and then a chicken for the pot. Dad would kill and pluck the bird and mum would draw it, a hangover from the time in her family's greengrocers and game shop. She didn't like it but did it. Food was much more seasonal in those days especially with their being few imports. The basic vegetables were potatoes, carrots, cabbage, sprouts and lettuce spring and summer. From time to time we would pick up a turnip that had fallen from a farm wagon. Fruit mostly meant apples – cooker or eaters and again only in season.

John and I were once invited to a birthday party where we saw our first orange. It was for a young boy who had come to live nearby. The family were a bit of a mystery. The boy had a cream pedal car in the style of a racing car and I think I was once allowed to sit in it. They seemed to have everything and the father was thought to be a 'spiv'; well dressed and nobody knew where he worked. It was said that if you were on the same bus as him, he would never get off at the same stop.

The only heating in the house was by means of coal fires. There was a built-in electric fire in each of the two larger bedrooms but they were seldom used because of the cost. Mostly we lived in the dining room as the fire there had a back boiler which provided hot water. In order to boost the hot water for a bath, a plate would be turned in the flue causing the fire to be drawn under the boiler with a consequent drop in heat into the room. The front room was rarely used. One exception was when John and I had chicken pox and beds were brought down and a fire lit to save mum running up and down stairs.

For a brief period, we had a displaced person staying with us. He was an elderly man from Sheffield I think with rather disgusting habits. He had been bombed out of his own home and although he had family, they were not prepared to accept him.

We continued to play 'gratey' – football with the grates in the kerbstones as goals. The days were long and double summertime made it difficult to sleep. Then one morning, I went into mum and dad's bedroom and he said 'It's all over'. I feel quite emotional recalling it now but I doubt if it meant much at the time. Come VE Day, grandma was staying with us and we went into York in the evening in dad's van. We parked on Piccadilly in front of the Regal Cinema. Grandma was most concerned that we would come back and find the van up on bricks with the wheels missing. She had heard of that happening in Leeds. She was greatly relieved when we found all four wheels on and we were able to drive home again.

Some time after VJ Day, there was a fancy dress parade at Museum Gardens. I went dressed as a joiner complete with apron, flat cap and a tool bag. ”

Name: Don Bullock
Born: 7 March 1933
Wartime location: Claylane, Mexborough

"For Bill Riley and I, 1941–43 wartime was a great era. We had the time of our lives. We ran free and it seemed that everyone else was old and miserable. With Dad away in the army, Mam working her fingers to the bone pegging rugs and cleaning at a local picture house to supplement the army pay, she was too occupied to keep tabs on me. Bill and I were as thick as thieves, always planning to do something that we shouldn't do. We had the run of Claylane (a row of terraced houses where we lived) from dawn to dusk – mischief was the name of our game.

Each street had its own gang. We were the Claylaners. Others were the Sparrow Barrackers, the Windhillers, the Pit Streeters and the most feared were the Denaby Ikes. When they attacked, we disappeared into the air raid shelters.

It just so happened that we were born in 1933, the year Hitler became Chancellor of Germany. Perhaps that had something to do with our behaviour! We used to call him Ickler or Shittlegruber. We had fun in the playground with our index fingers of our left hands over our top lips and right hands outstretched, taking long strides and shouting: 'Hile Hickler! Actung this is funf speaking.'

Lots of people look back and say just how trying life in wartime was . . . but for me and Bill it gave us cover in the darkness and we enjoyed the searchlights playing the night skies.

Kids played kick-can, hopscotch, hidey, relieve-ho, tiggy, peggy, marbles etc., loads of games in the streets, but that was never enough for us. We lit grass fires, stole lead from outside toilets to melt it down, threw stones at windows (not our own), collected birds' nests, climbed the chapel and Doncaster Road school roofs, played in the sewage works, and paddled in the reed beds with our boots slung on our necks by the laces when wagging it from school.

We made barrows and bikes albeit without tyres, brakes, seats or chains. All our material came from regular evening excursions to the local tip. We used to find all sorts on the tip. Bottles to return to the beer-off (penny refund). We found marbles and sometimes coins in slurry that had been dumped after roadside drains had been emptied. Sometimes we used to take Peggy and Nigger with us – two of the dogs that lived down the lane. They made the rats squeal – the tip was overrun with them.

The grass field opposite Clayfield Lane was fired many times. Once we got a fire going, we let it spread on say a twenty yard front and controlled the direction it took with our jackets – same jackets we wore for school or to catch butterflies with. We made fires to roast potatoes stolen from the farmer's field. We also stole turnips (tongees). You weren't a Claylaner if you never did these things. At potato picking time, the farm hand used to walk alongside the carthorse concentrating on guiding it through the ruts the channels of rainwater had carved out. We would lay in hiding and as soon as the horse passed, we'd jump up the back of the cart to pull spuds off.

We weren't bad all the time. We had our good points. There were times when we'd run from school at home time, rush down the pastures and help farm labourer Horace Finney walk the cows up from the meadow to Louis Latham's farm for milking. Very rarely did we go straight home from school. Another time when we wanted to be good lads, we took flowers for our teacher Miss Dennet; in retrospect she must have suspected that we stole them from Castle Hill Park. A two-ton cannon stood by the bandstand on the Castle Hill and Bill and I thought it would be better in our back yard. So we stole Auntie Mary's clothes line, tied it to the cannon and we were trying our best to tow it away when the park keeper Old Middleton chased us away.

Some people on the lane kept a pig or a goose, hen or cockerel to supplement food rationing. One day, Mam gave me 7s 6d and told me to go to the poultry farm on Church Street and ask for a six-month old pullet on the point of lay. Bill and I planned otherwise. Instead of buying one, it would be easier to pinch one and share the 7s 6d.

We knew where to go – we'd seen them when birds' nesting at Mexborough Low Locks. We also knew that the lock keeper, Old Woody, only had one eye and figured that was to our advantage.

Woody's locks were a mile away and for the first half mile we walked on the towpath behind a horse towing a barge. We reached the pit overhead ropeway system, climbed the vertical twenty-five feet high steel ladder and stepped off onto the wire meshing that spanned the canal. It was a safety net to protect barges from falling debris as slag buckets passed over. We were quickly over and down the other side and had Woody's hens in sight. They were free range in a field by the pen. We chased them around until we cornered one, wrapped it in my jacket and took turns to carry it home. We installed it in the coalhouse. Job well done!

On seeing it, Mam blew a fuse and asked for the change as cocks were only 5s and she told me to take it back and ask for a pullet or 2s 6d change. We were quick to respond. We made our way to Tommy Coggin's farm, stole lots of eggs and placed them in with the cockerel. We told

1. 'Will they come?' Defender's eye-view of an invasion beach from a pill box. *(LMA)*

Daily Mail

NORTHCLIFFE HOUSE, LONDON, E.C.4.

Telephone: CENTRAL 6000.

4th September, 1939. 247th Day.

WAR

11a.m., September 3rd, 1939

Great Britain and France are at war with Germany. We now fight against the blackest tyranny that has ever held men in bondage. We fight to defend, and to restore, freedom and justice on earth.

Let us face the truth. This war was inevitable whether it began with Austria, Sudetenland, Bohemia, or Danzig. If it had not come over Danzig it would have come later upon some other issue.

It became inevitable from the day Hitler seized power in Germany and began his criminal career by enslaving all others by the methods of brute force.

Once more Britain, her Empire, and her friends are engaged in a conflict to uphold Right against Might. If the democracies had flinched now they would have been compelled to abdicate for ever their title to be called the champions of liberty. The fate of those small nations who have already lost their rights would have been theirs in turn.

This was the dominant thought in the inspiring message broadcast by the King to his people last night. We go to war because we must. In his Majesty's words: 'For the sake of all that we ourselves hold dear, and of the world's order and peace, it is unthinkable that we should refuse to meet the challenge.'

2. Editorial in the Daily Mail, 4 September 1939. *(Daily Mail)*

WANTED!

FOR MURDER . . . FOR KIDNAPPING . . .

FOR THEFT AND FOR ARSON

Can be recognised full face by habitual scowl. Rarely smiles. Talks rapidly, and when angered screams like a child.

ADOLF HITLER

ALIAS

Adolf Schicklegruber,

Adolf Hittler or Hidler

Last heard of in Berlin, September 3, 1939. Aged fifty, height 5ft. 8½in., dark hair, frequently brushes one lock over left forehead. Blue eyes. Sallow complexion, stout build, weighs about 11st. 3lb. Suffering from acute monomania, with periodic fits of melancholia. Frequently bursts into tears when crossed. Harsh, guttural voice, and has a habit of raising right hand to shoulder level. DANGEROUS!

Profile from a recent photograph. Black moustache. Jowl inclines to fatness. Wide nostrils. Deep-set, menacing eyes.

FOR MURDER Wanted for the murder of over a thousand of his fellow countrymen on the night of the Blood Bath, June 30, 1934. Wanted for the murder of countless political opponents in concentration camps.

He is indicted for the murder of Jews, Germans, Austrians, Czechs, Spaniards and Poles. He is now urgently wanted for homicide against citizens of the British Empire.

Hitler is a gunman who shoots to kill. He acts first and talks afterwards.

No appeals to sentiment can move him. This gangster, surrounded by armed hoodlums, is a natural killer. The reward for his apprehension, dead or alive, is the peace of mankind.

FOR KIDNAPPING Wanted for the kidnapping of Dr. Kurt Schuschnigg, late Chancellor of Austria. Wanted for the kidnapping of Pastor Niemoller, a heroic martyr who was not afraid to put God before Hitler. Wanted for the attempted kidnapping of Dr. Benes, late President of Czechoslovakia. The kidnapping tendencies of this established criminal are marked and violent. The symptoms before an attempt are threats, blackmail and ultimatums. He offers his victims the alternatives of complete surrender or timeless incarceration in the horrors of concentration camps.

FOR THEFT Wanted for the larceny of eighty millions of Czech gold in March, 1939. Wanted for the armed robbery of material resources of the Czech state. Wanted for the stealing of Memelland. Wanted for robbing mankind of peace, of humanity, and for the attempted assault on civilisation itself. This dangerous lunatic masks his raids by spurious appeals to honour, to patriotism and to duty. At the moment when his protestations of peace and friendship are at their most vehement, he is most likely to commit his smash and grab.

His tactics are known and easily recognised. But Europe has already been wrecked and plundered by the depredations of this armed thug who smashes in without scruple.

FOR ARSON Wanted as the incendiary who started the Reichstag fire on the night of February 27, 1933. This crime was the key point, and the starting signal for a series of outrages and brutalities that are unsurpassed in the records of criminal degenerates. As a direct and immediate result of this calculated act of arson, an innocent dupe, Van der Lubbe, was murdered in cold blood. But as an indirect outcome of this carefully-planned offence, Europe itself is ablaze. The fires that this man has kindled cannot be extinguished until he himself is apprehended—dead or alive!

THIS RECKLESS CRIMINAL IS WANTED—DEAD OR ALIVE!

3. Wanted poster for the most infamous man alive. Strangely, there was no price on his head. Would bounty hunters have grabbed him for £1 million? *(LMA)*

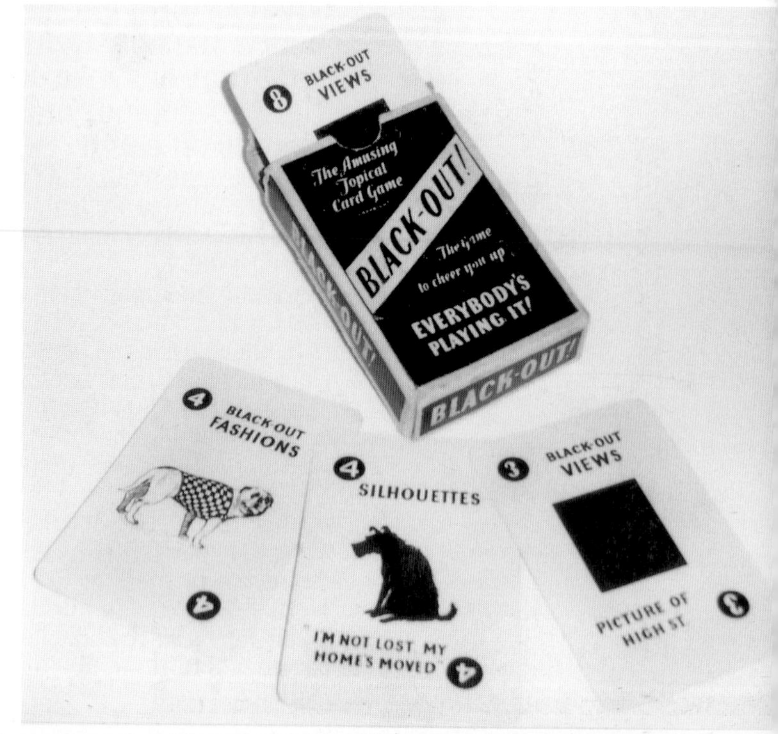

4. 'Black Out!' was a popular 1940s parlour game. *(www.how-we-lived-then.co.uk)*

5. Boys were encouraged to make models of patriotic national symbols of might and majesty. HMS *Hood* was sunk in the Battle of Denmark Strait on 24 May 1941 but Buckingham Palace remained miraculously unmolested. *(www.how-we-lived-then.co.uk)*

6. Government icon showing conformity with economy standards. *(LMA)*

7. 'Dig For Victory' posters were found on every street corner. *(LMA)*

7. Ivy Shears could only dream of a cake like this. It was made by Charlie Hitchen at a cost of just one guinea. He is still waiting payment! (see OF BAKERS AND CONFECTIONERS). *(Charlie Hitchen)*

8. Detail of Ration Book and wartime coins. *(LMA)*

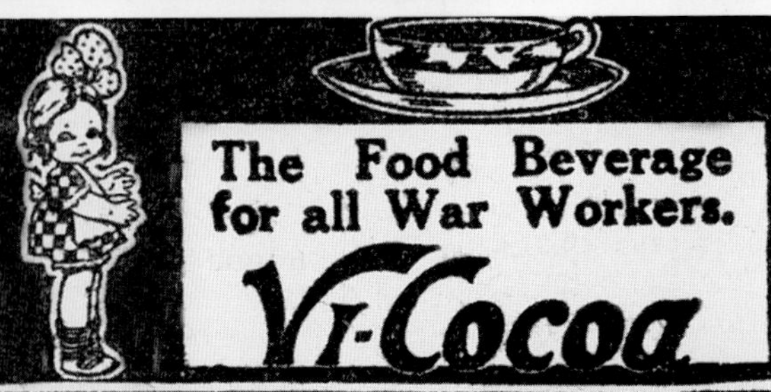

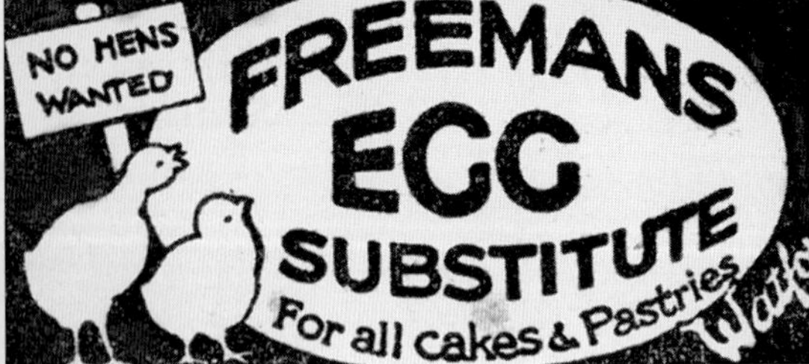

9. The term 'taking a powder' took on a whole new meaning during the war. *(LMA)*

BLACKOUT

NEARLY 1,200 KILLED IN DECEMBER ALONE

Don't think that accidents only happen to other people. Tonight on *your* way home there will be danger. Don't step off the kerb without looking both ways. Throw the light of your torch down on the ground so that you do not dazzle drivers. You cannot risk taking *any* chances.

10. Blackout posters such as this could not be seen in the dark. *(LMA)*

THE DAILY MAIL

TUESDAY, JUNE 6, 1944. THREE HALFPENCE

OUR ARMIES IN N. FRANCE

4,000 INVASION SHIPS HAVE CROSSED CHANNEL

BRITISH AND CANADIANS SECURE 2 BEACHHEADS

GERMANS SAY TANKS LANDED NEAR CAEN IN NORMANDY

DELIVERANCE DAY has dawned. The great Allied invasion for the liberation of Europe began early this morning when Allied armies, under the supreme command of General Eisenhower, started to land on the northern coast of France. Already British and Canadian troops have secured beachheads at ... points and dug in, while a German report says that tanks have been landed in the area of Arromanches (20 miles N.W. of Caen on the Normandy coast).

"Under the command of General Eisenhower Allied naval forces, supported by strong air forces, began landing Allied armies this morning on the northern coast of France."

IMMENSE ARMADA

The Premier said that massed airborne landings have been successfully effected behind the enemy's lines. The landings on the beaches are proceeding at various points at the present time. The fire of the shore batteries has been largely quelled.

GOING TO PLAN

So far the commanders who are engaged report that everything is proceeding according to plan, he said. And what a plan. This vast operation is undoubtedly the most complicated and difficult which has ever occurred.

The landings, it is understood in London, were made in Normandy between 6 a.m. and 8.15 a.m., minesweepers clearing a way. Naval bombardments, in which U.S. battleships took part, were carried out and airborne landings made, first reports being described as "good."

FRENCHMEN WARNED

Latest German claims are that at least four Anglo-American parachute and airborne divisions are engaged, that the airborne landings in Normandy have been made in great depth, and that a "big Allied warship" has been set on fire.

Massed Bomber Fleet

'THE INVASION HAS BEGUN'

—BERLIN

Airborne Troops Land in Seine Estuary

Atlantic Wall in Action

The King to Broadcast

Allies Land on Channel Islands

Allies Speed Up Chase North of Rome

Stretching His Fighters

Hull Invasion Springboard

Waves of Assaulting Infantry

Splendid Troops

Liberation of Rome

Massed Airborne Landings Behind Enemy's Lines

—MR CHURCHILL

BEACHES STORMED: FIRE OF SHORE BATTERIES LARGELY QUELLED

THE Prime Minister reported to the House of Commons on the progress of the great battle now being waged in France. He said:

Relentless Pursuit

'This Vast Plan'

The Breakthrough

Oslo Not Heard

+RED CROSS COMPETITIONS

to help our wounded and prisoners of war

Thousands of games and sports contests are being arranged all over the country in aid of our prisoners of war. Any game is suitable and the Red Cross Sports Committee provide the PRIZES, Score Cards, Posters, Admission Tickets and Entry Forms.

DARTS · TABLE TENNIS
SNOOKER · BILLIARDS
WHIST DRIVES · BRIDGE

11. The front page of the *Hull Daily Mail* for 6 June 1944. *(LMA)*

12. In January 1940, snowfall was particularly bad in the Dales. *(LMA)*

No more flying off the handle

— since taking Phosferine says this teacher.

Monmouthshire.

"I am a teacher by profession and find Phosferine very useful in combating the 'end of term feeling' and relieving nerve strain. It soothes frayed nerves and prevents one 'flying off the handle' over trifles. Some time ago I avoided a nervous breakdown with the help of Phosferine."

Yours faithfully,
(Miss) R.E.W.

Take 10 drops or 2 Tablets
Two Tablets equal ten drops

10 drops will put new heart into you!

when you are feeling in need of a Tonic

Your first dose of Phosferine will bring you valuable benefit within fifteen minutes. Ten drops will buck you up. And every succeeding dose will put back into you what overwork, worry or illness have taken out—strength, energy, vitality. Phosferine will put new heart into you, restore your confidence. It will help you resist winter ailments and give you the good health you need to meet the strain of days like these. Ask your chemist for a bottle of this really great tonic today.

PHOSFERINE (*Tablets or Liquid*), **1/5, 3/5, 5/8,** (*Including Purchase Tax*)
Two Tablets equal ten drops of Liquid. The 3/5 size is nearly four times the 1/5 size; you save 2/-

PHOSFERINE

THE GREATEST OF ALL TONICS *Bran*

—for—	—for—	—for—	—for—
Depression	Brain Fag	Influenza	Anæmia
Headache	Neuralgia	Rheumatism	Debility
Indigestion	Sleeplessness	Sciatica	Neurasthenia

WARNING. THE PUBLIC IS WARNED AGAINST PURCHASING WORTHLESS IMITATION

13. Why weren't barrel-fulls offered to the military? The war would have been won by Christmas. *(LMA)*

14. Even Yorkshire's Bertie Bassett did his bit. *(LMA)*

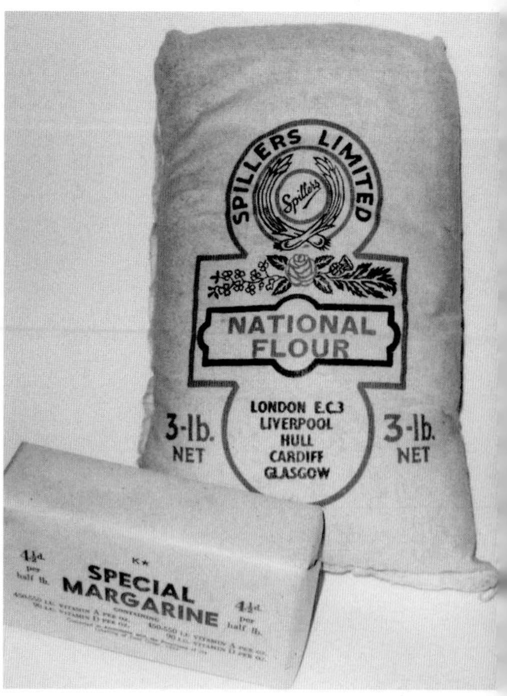

15. Like it or lump it, these were the nation staples. *(www.how-we-lived-then.co.uk)*

16. Anxious and bewildered Bevin Boys on their first shift at Markham Main in 1943. *(Brian Elliott)*

17. Harold Jackson (furthest left) and other Bevin Boys outside their Sandringham Road Nissen hut hostel. *(Brian Elliott)*

18. Colin Massingham still has his old miner's helmet. *(Brian Elliott)*

19. Ex- Bevin Boy Joe Hartley worked for many years as a Deputy at Manvers Main. *(Brian Elliott)*

20. Wartime advert for a popular men's hair cream. *(LMA)*

21. Graphic wartime railway poster. *(LMA)*

22. Walter Salmon (second from left) on the footplate of a steam engine in the 1930s. *(Hilary B Blackburne)*

COD STEAK, 1s. 6d. A LB. TO-DAY, MAY BE SCARCE

By Daily Mail Reporter

IF cod is scarce in the shops to-day—first day of fixed maximum prices for Iceland cod—do not blame the control scheme. It is probably due to circumstances beyond the control of the fishing industry which has introduced the scheme voluntarily.

"Many shoppers will be able to get Iceland cod, and possibly below the control price, too," a leading merchant told me last night, "but in some districts it may be scarce.

"We hope plentiful supplies will soon be available."

Top Prices

Maximum prices now are: Cod steaks 1s. 6d. per lb., cod fillets 1s. 10d. unskinned, 2s. skinned, cured fillets skinned 2s. 2d., codling 1s. 8d.

In many parts of the country on Saturday cod steaks could be bought at 1s. 6d. per lb., though during the winter the prices ranged from 2s. to 3s.

Biggest question in the industry is how the allocation scheme will operate at the ports.

Auction sales will be conducted as usual, but merchants will be allowed only to buy up to their quota, and bidding will cease when the price-at-port maximum has been reached.

More Control

As soon as the industry is able to perfect the scheme for Iceland cod, which represents about 60 per cent. of our fish supplies, meetings are to be held with the Food Ministry to discuss fixing maximum prices for other kinds of fish.

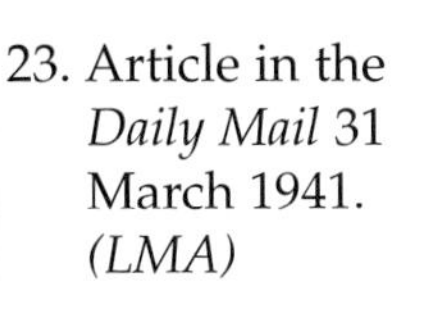

23. Article in the *Daily Mail* 31 March 1941. *(LMA)*

24. Between trips, fishermen would relax in the pub (reconstruction at the Grimsby Fishing Museum). *(LMA)*

25. Wartime re-enactment scene at Pickering Station (LNER A2 Pacific 4-6-2 engine 60532 *'Blue Peter'* entered service with British Railways in 1948). *(LMA)*

26. Boys from St Peter's School, York enjoying a mid-harvest break on a farm at Coulton near Hovingham in August 1944. Roger Frost is the second from right. *(Roger Frost)*

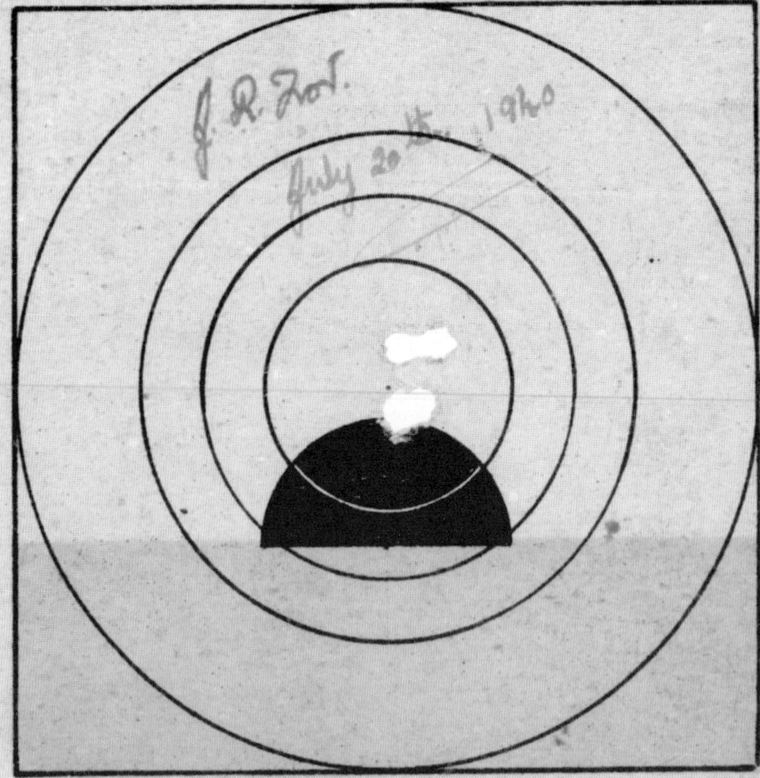

27. St Peter's School Cadet Force had its own rifle range. Crack shot Roger Frost hit five bulls eyes on 20 July 1940. *(Roger Frost)*

28. Harvest time at Holme-on-Spalding Moor. *(LMA)*

29. A stalwart group of young Civil Defence Volunteers (Dennis Simpson is on the back row, far right). *(Mrs S Simpson)*

30. York was bombed on the night of 28/29 Apri 1942 in retaliation for a terror attack in Lübeck. St Peter's School was damaged in the raid. *(St Peter's School, York)*

31. The wartime road to Spurn Point has crumbled away. *(LMA)*

32. Constance Millington helping with the harvest in Bakewell, Derbyshire. *(Rita Hartley)*

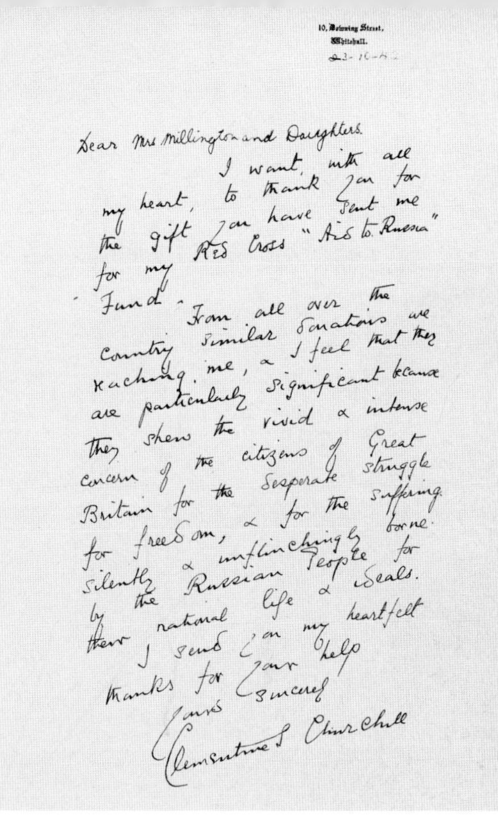

10, Downing Street,
Whitehall.
23-10-4[illegible]

Dear Mrs Millington and Daughters.

I want, with all my heart, to thank you for the gift you have sent me for my Red Cross "Aid to Russia" Fund.

From all over the country similar donations are reaching me, & I feel that they are particularly significant because they shew the vivid & intense concern of the citizens of Great Britain for the desperate struggle for freedom, & for the suffering silently & unflinchingly borne by the Russian people for their national life & ideals.

I send you my heartfelt thanks for your help

Yours sincerely

Clementine S Churchill

33. Letter of thanks sent by the Prime Minister's wife Clementine Churchill to Mrs Constance Millington. *(Rita Hartley)*

34. Most domestic Anderson shelters were less sophisticated than this reconstruction. *(LMA)*

35. 'Doh ah uck gud i is?' (the author tries on a gas mask for size). *(LMA)*

36. Wartime gravy advertisement in a local newspaper. *(LMA)*

37. Hull evacuees attending Bishop Wilton School, Bishop Wilton New York. *(Mike Pratt)*

38. Bishop Wilton from Stonetable Hill. *(LMA)*

39. Evacuee John Crathern with his foster parents George and Ethel Bedford. *(John Crathern)*

40. Portrait of Will Pickles in the Royal College of General Practitioners, London. *(LMA/RCGP)*

41. Aysgarth. *(LMA)*

42. Addeborough from Nappa Scar. *(LMA)*

43. Before she leaves for work, a Red Cross nurse enjoys her breakfast in the wartime kitchen. *(www.how-we-live-then.co.uk)*

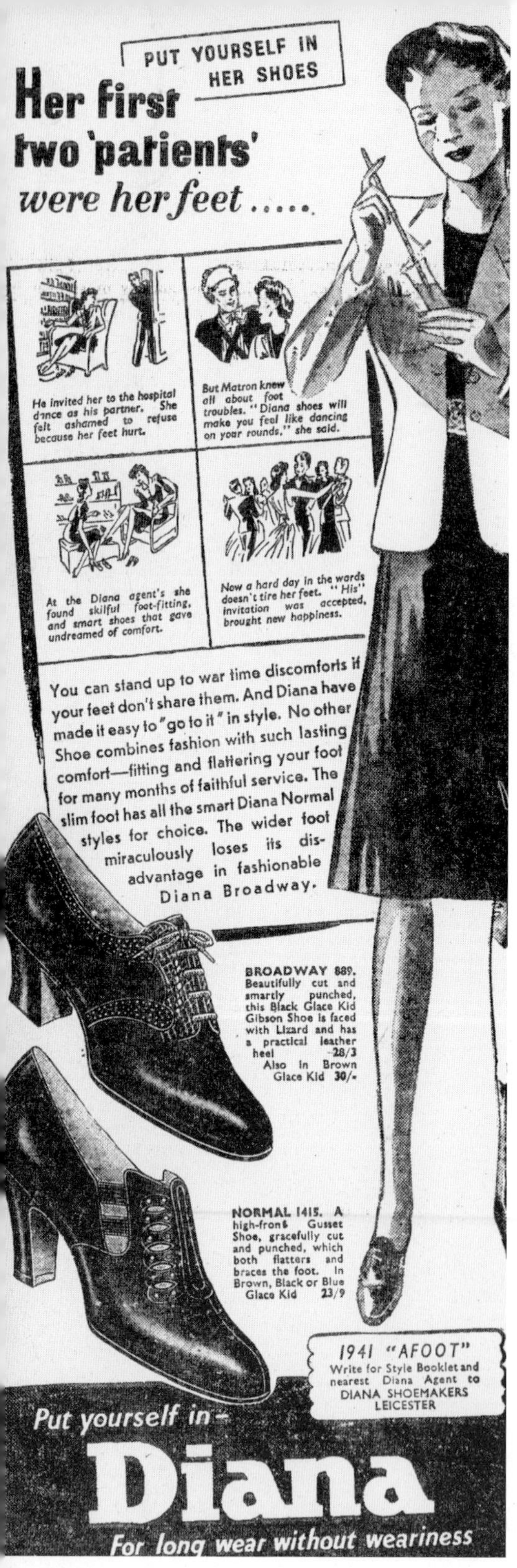

44. These shoes 'make you feel like dancing on your rounds': *Daily Mail*, 31 March 1941.

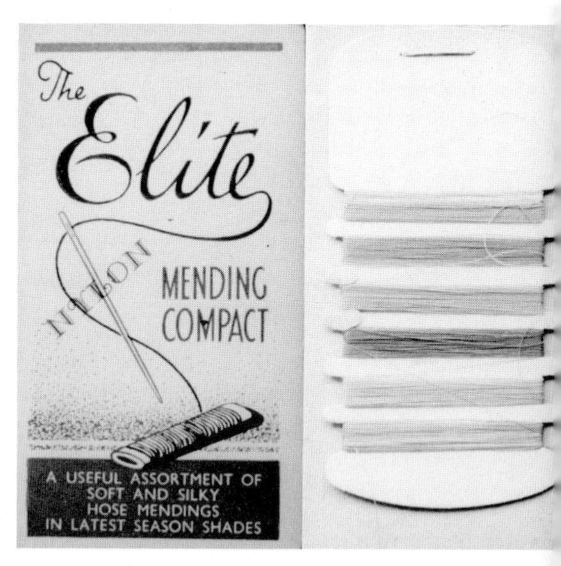

45. Ladders posed no fears for girls who had sweethearts...others had to resort to this. *(LMA)*

46. This pill-box on Fraisthorpe Beach was constructed just a short distance from the Megginson's farm. *(LMA)*

47. Charlie Hitchen with his little handcart (the cardboard boxes on top contained loaves and teacakes). *(Charlie Hitchen)*

48. Charlie Hitchen and his Morris delivery van. *(Charlie Hitchen)*

49. Charlie Hitchen and his wife Violet outside the Junction House Bakery. *(Charlie Hitchen)*

C. HITCHIN

JUNCTION HOUSE, HOLMFIRTH | **HADE EDGE, Telephone 471**

With Compliments of the Season

For delivery Friday, December 24th, 1954

Large Loaves	Coconut Cream Sandwich, 2s. ....
Small Loaves	Orange Cream Sandwich, 2s. ....
Sliced Loaves	Lemon Cream Sandwich, 2s. ....
Brown Loaves	Choc. Iced Sandwich, 1s. 6d. ....
Plain Teacakes	Short Lemon Tarts, 2½d. ....
Sultana Teacakes	Short Jam Tarts, 2½d. ....
Large Plain Teacakes	Puff Lemon Tarts, 2½d. ....
Large Sultana Teacakes	Puff Jam Tarts, 2½d. ....
Brown Teacakes	Puff Cream Tarts, 2½d. ....
Chocolate Logs, 3s.	Puff Jam Turnovers, 2½d. ....
Chocolate Rolls, 1s. 6d.	Short Mince Pies, 3d. ....
Jam Rolls, 1s. 6d.	Puff Mince Pies, 3d. ....
Lemon Rolls, 1s. 6d.	Ground Rice Tarts, 2½d. ....
Parkin Loaf, 1s. 6d.	Cream Buns, 2½d. ....
Cherry Loaf, 1s. 6d.	Iced Buns, 3d. ....
Seed Loaf, 1s. 6d.	Cherry Slices, 2½d. ....
Madeira Loaf, 1s. 6d.	Coconut Slices, 2½d. ....
Coconut Loaf, 1s. 6d.	Madeleines, 3d. ....
Currant Loaf, 2s.	Sponge Drops, 3d. ....
Walnut Cream Sandwich, 2s. 4d.	Marble Squares, 2½d. ....
Cream Sandwich, 2s.	Iced Currant Pasties, 3d. ....
Jam Sandwich, 1s. 6d.	Currant Buns, 2½d. ....
Lemon Sandwich, 1s. 6d.	Viennese Tarts, 2½d. ....
Coffee Cream Sandwich, 2s.	Almond Tarts, 3d. ....
Jam and Coconut Cream Sandwich, 2s.	Scones, 2½d. ....

Collins and Co. Ltd., Printers, "Express" Office, Holmfirth

50. Charlie Hitchen's Christmas Price List, 1954. *(Charlie Hitchen)*

51. Barbara Rawson, aged five in 1944. *(Barbara Pettitt)*

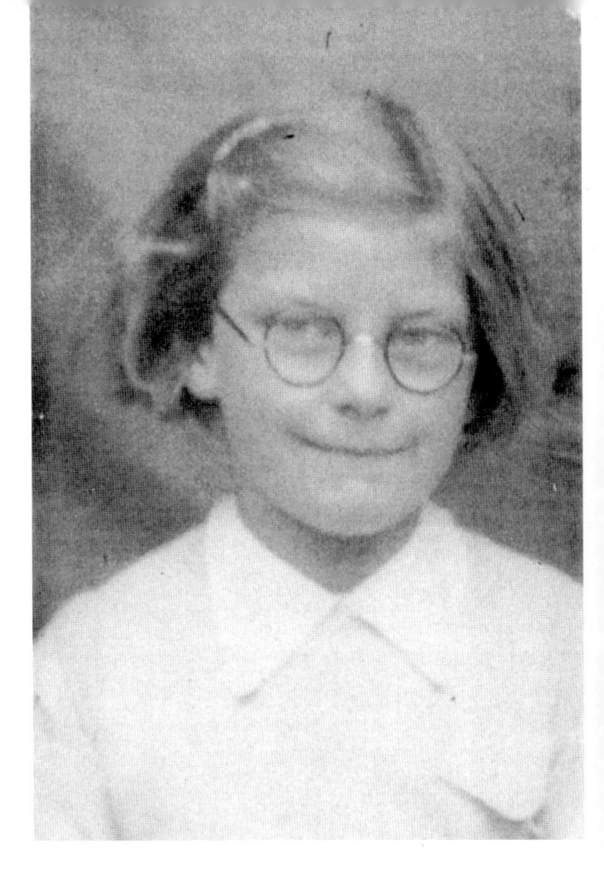

52. Most servicemen did not own a fountain pen. My father's letters home were written in pencil. *(LMA)*

53. Photograph of the author's mother and sister dated 5 June 1943. Inscribed 'To my darling Husband from Ethel'. Posted to the author's father who was on active service with the Royal Navy. *(LMA)*

Even when it's
NO SMOKING
by Order

Why worry?

When your throat's kept soothed by the fruit in Rowntree's Gums and Pastilles you won't bother too much about the cigarettes you can't smoke. Long-lasting and refreshing — they really do taste of fruit! Rowntree's Gums and Pastilles might have been invented specially for this war and its weary hours of no-smoking duties.

ROWNTREE'S FRUIT CLEAR GUMS

refresh & soothe

2d TUBES
3d & 6d PACKETS

Mixed Clear Gums (Hard — long-lasting). Mixed Pastilles (Sugar-coated — softer)

54. Wartime advertisement for Rowntree's Fruit Gums. *(LMA)*

55. Dennis and Doris Bedford. *(Barry Bedford)*

56. Home Guard Robert Markham in 1942 at the rear of Daisy Hill (Drax Church spire is just visible in the background). *(Robert Markham)*

57. Hilda Appleby in 1923 (The location is probably Filey Brigg). *(Mrs J. Mordue)*

58. Wartime re-enactment scene at Pickering Station. *(LMA)*

59. Recruitment poster for Women's Land Army. *(LMA)*

60. Land Army rat-catchers spooning out bait in Barwick-in-Elmet. *(LMA)*

61. Under-the-stairs essentials for dealing with the aftermath of bombing – ARP jackets, hard hats, candles, air-raid instruction manual, gas masks, lantern, anti-gas ointment, tea flask, a bell and warden's wooden rattle (marked B & E Co ARP 1939). *(www.how-we-lived-then.co.uk)*

62. Raymond Peat in his uniform. *(Raymond Peat)*

63. Alfred Dunning.
(Brian Dunning)

64. In his spare time Alfred Dunning was a prolific amateur artist but according to his son, 'never sold anything'. This evocative study is of Whitby Harbour.
(Brian Dunning)

Cameraman's Story Was as Good as His Pictures

J. H. Magee, *Picture Post* cameraman, was recently on an assignment aboard a cruiser on convoy duty in the Mediterranean. He took some very fine photographs and wrote a short account of his trip. This was to have been rewritten, but the account was so vivid that it was used in its original form. Pictures and story are in the current issue.

During the trip the sudden opening of an action caught him unawares—he had forgotten his earplugs and anti-flash headgear. He witnessed the destruction of an attacking plane by a lone Liberator and describes the running commentary given for the benefit of those below deck.

During the following raids one bomb fell within 20 yards of the ship, but he instinctively pressed the trigger and secured a fine "shot." The gunfire was so great, he says, that it benumbed his mind, and it was instinct alone which kept him holding the camera at the alert.

65. Newspaper article about Hayward Magee's Picture Post assignment. *(Mrs A Oura)*

66. Haywood Magee. *(Mrs A Oura)*

No. 73 P.o.W. Camp
Stoorwood
December 1947.

Dear Mr. and Mrs. Smith,

I feel I must send you a personal note of thanks for your kindness. My knowledge of English is not great enough to express everything I want to say, therefore a friend of mine translated my letter from German ito English. I wish you all a happy Christmas. Christmas is to me as to all real Christians in the world a feast of love and peace. It should be peace amongst all nations in the whole world, because every Country needs peace. Having spent five years off home, it is a great honour to spend Christmas with you. I wish to thank you most sincerely for the kind interest you were good enoug to extend to me. Of course five years is a long time especially if you are par-ted from your dear family, and I shall be really glad when I am re-united. I remember with pleasure past years I had spent peacefully at home. Before the war I had a good job, was satis-fied and lived happily. But memory is all I have got. Life is not easy, as we say in German "Ohne Fleiss kein Preis." (proverb) I lost much during the war, things which ware dear and valuable, but they're gone for ever. I don't complain about as I got still confidence to re-start a new life under uncertain conditions, and there will come happy days once more. I am P.o.W. three and a half years already, you probably won't realize what that means. A man behind barbed-wire is expelled from the human party, he is just a number on any sheet and he only exists in ledgers, he is a source of man-power and doesn't lead an individual life. Therefore a P.o.W. has different views as a free person. It is easy to make a Prisoner satisfied and happy, he is full of joy about anything and keeps everything longer as other people do. We are grateful and don't forget good deeds. I could write a lot about our sorrows but I will not waste paper. I shall always remember with great pleasure the time spent on your farm, hop-ing you were satisfied with me. My one regret is I cannot work for you any longer. I feel I cannot speak too highly of what you have done for me. Working for you has been throughout a source of interest and enjoy-ment. I know, there was a lot still to be done but I can't help. I am sorry as I could not do everything as I liked to do, especially the things for Christmas because there was a shortage of material.

But what I have made I did carefully, intending to please you. I don't know wother or not I get time to pay a visit to you before I leave your island, therefore once again accept my thanks for everything. When I learned I must leave you I had tears in my eyes, I shall keep you in my memory for ever. When I arrive at home I don't know yet where to stay and what to do. If you like you can write me a letter I should like at any time. Closing that note with all the best to you all, wish-ing you every success in farming. My kind regards to Betty, Lilian, Dorothy, Ernest, and George,

Yours very sincerely
Friedrich Heinmann

67. Fred Heinmann's farewell letter to the Smith family. *(Ernest Smith)*

8th June, 1946

TO-DAY, AS WE CELEBRATE VICTORY, I send this personal message to you and all other boys and girls at school. For you have shared in the hardships and dangers of a total war and you have shared no less in the triumph of the Allied Nations.

I know you will always feel proud to belong to a country which was capable of such supreme effort; proud, too, of parents and elder brothers and sisters who by their courage, endurance and enterprise brought victory. May these qualities be yours as you grow up and join in the common effort to establish among the nations of the world unity and peace.

George R.I.

68. Proclamation sent to schoolchildren at the end of hostilities. *(LMA)*

Mam to come and look, the hen has laid some eggs! She was having none of it and next day we took the cock back and pinched one that didn't have long tail feathers.

Bill Riley, my mate, was one of ten children. Bill was on the small side. He could curl up on the inside of a lorry tyre. I know you will find this hard to take in, but it is absolutely true. We would wheel the tyre up the slope of the main road. Bill would get curled up inside it and I helped him on his way. He would leave the road at a slight bend, come to a stop in an open field and topple out as the tyre collapsed ... laughing. There was very little traffic in those days. You could lie down and go to sleep in the road. Bill was very daring and feared nothing. He used to climb the cast iron fall pipes of houses, then grab hold of the gutter and move along hanging by his hands to retrieve lost tennis balls. ❞

(The entry above, which is included with the kind permission of the author, is an edited extract – with additions – from an article entitled 'Reflections of Two Rogues' that appeared in the magazine *Down Your Way* in November 2005)

After leaving school at the age of fourteen at the end of the Christmas term in 1946, Don started work in a local brickworks. But, despite having little money and despite the continuing problems of rationing, he continued his adventures, planning his post war trip of a lifetime with three pals – Arnie, Reg and his old friend Bill. He takes up the story:

❝ We were intrigued with the map of England that belonged to Reg. We looked at all the towns we could go to on our bikes and guessed the distances, deciding, for some reason, on Blackpool. We'd all heard of it. We all knew it had a tower and it was a seaside town and it didn't seem all that far on the map. So it was a unanimous decision. We'd go for the weekend. That evening, we went for a training spin.

Bill's was the family bike made up of bits of this and that. Arnie's was a fixed gear type, which meant that he'd have to peddle all the time. Little did we know it would be ninety-eight miles to Blackpool. Reg's bike was a 28-inch wheel of Hercules make. My bike was a Phillips 26-inch wheel with Sturmey Archer three speed gears. I bought it from Wigfalls in Mexborough for £15. At 5 shillings a week, it would take sixty weeks to pay it off and 5 shillings was my pocket money out of my wages at the time.

We all gave work a miss on the Saturday for an early start. We peddled like mad to keep up with each other and, going down hills, Arnie had to keep peddling being fixed gear. Reg's expertise in map reading got us to

Halifax where the hills were getting higher and longer. We had some help on the rising ground by tagging on to the tail ends of heavily ladened wool lorries. How Arnie coped with tagging on, I don't know. On some down hills, he used to step off the pedals and spread his legs outwards letting the pedals whiz round. We stopped at a Pennine roadside cabin where we bought a drink and rested awhile. We were the only ones there. It was like being on the moon in 1947. We guessed from the map that we were at half way and we might as well continue. Further on, we went over a line painted across the road. It said 'Yorkshire' on one side and 'Lancashire' on the other. After peddling on and talking among ourselves about this line, we decided to go back to the Yorkshire side and walk across the line into Lancashire so that we could tell them back home that we walked from Yorkshire into Lancashire.

When we tried to step down from our bikes on the sea front by the tower, our backsides were really sore. We could only walk with the aid of our bikes as props. My legs bowed outwards at the knees and we were very hungry. We each bought a cream cake and leant on the railings to eat them. A chap with a box camera took our photos and within a short time, we set off back to Mexborough.

After doing over twenty miles past Preston, night was almost upon us. We went into a field of very tall grass and lay down in a heap, falling asleep by the side of our bikes. At the break of dawn, with dew on our faces, we saw what appeared to be an orchard. The grass was too tall to push our bikes through, so we left them and off we went scrumping. Only thing was that the trees were bare. It was too early in the year. A chap yelled out to us and we scampered. He must have been surprised to see we had bikes. We peddled away leaving him looking on. Going downhill in Todmorden, Bill's brake cable dropped from his handlebar into his front wheel, bouncing Bill into a shop window. Bill wasn't easily hurt – nothing bothered him – and after fixing his brake, we were back on track towards Halifax and home.

Later in the day after a short rest and a feed, we were back on our bikes heading for the east coast, arriving in Bridlington before dark. A fishmonger gave us permission to sleep in his fish storage yard on top of the empty wooden wet fish boxes. An early morning start back to Mexborough enabled me to get to work in the afternoon for a 12.30 start after the works dinner break.

We four crossed the Pennines from the west coast to the east coast in the same day . . . but ooh . . . that bloody saddle. ”

Name: Geoffrey Pallister
Born: 9 June 1932
Wartime location: Nunthorpe Road, York and Spurn Point

"I was just seven years old when war broke out. I was in Yearsley Bridge Isolation Hospital with diphtheria. My mum worked on the railway station and made friends with a woman I called Aunt Gert who lived in Leeman Road. She had a daughter who was the same age as my sister. They were both pains in the neck and wanted to go everywhere with me. We used to spend weeks at Aunt Gert's when we had to walk to school each morning through what was known as the Marble Arch. It was about 400 yards long. One section was for traffic and the other was a walk through. It was built up with sandbags on alternate sides every ten yards so you didn't know what was round the next corner. It was very scary and was also used for an air raid shelter.

Lil White was also a friend of mum's. Occasionally, they'd go to the Hop Grove Inn and then back to Lil's for a singsong and would bring back soldiers for pie and peas. I didn't like them bringing back the soldiers. I used to think of my dad fighting in Greece and these lads having a good time with our girls. I remember one lad going back to camp one night was run over and killed by a van. I felt glad – maybe I shouldn't have, but it felt like justice at the time.

I was ten years old when we had the big bombing raid over York*. My sister and I were under the kitchen table. I remember a massive explosion and our old Yorkist range must have moved out about a foot and back again. The room was filled with soot and dust just like a thick fog – we were all like chimney sweeps and even to this day when a siren goes off my mouth tastes of soot. Uncle Bob took us round to our grans – I was in pyjamas and had Uncle Bob's army tin hat on. When we came out of our house, the houses opposite were on fire; bricks, slates, glass and dust were all over the road. But the worst of all was the crying and screaming of our neighbours. One of our school friends was killed. She and her family were in the shelter and the concrete roof was blown off killing Betty. She was the same age as me. Her mum never got over Betty's death. She used to shout at my mum 'that it was not fair that she had lost Betty and my mum still had the two of you'.

When mum saw what the house was like she said: 'Right we're going to your dad.' He was in the Catering Corp stationed at – wait for it – Spurn Point! When we got off the train at Hull, I thought we were in Hell. As far as I could see, all the town centre was on fire. We got to Patrington and lived in a gypsy caravan in a field next to the post office.

School was my problem throughout the war. On Spurn, each village had its own school so, as we moved with dad's job, we moved schools. The teachers always seemed to put me next to a girl I hated. I'd ask to go to the toilet and I'd be off! I'd go anywhere. On the farms to help them with the pea pulling or just on the small area of beach that was not mined. I used to hate gardening being a towny. I didn't know a hoe from a rake. The local lads used to make fun of me. I was a loner.

The last place we stayed at was the *Crown and Cushion* pub at the end of Spurn Point. My sister and I had to go to school with two or three local children by horse and cart. By now, I realised if I didn't go to school on the first day, the teacher didn't know I existed. So at this school, I'd get on the cart outside the pub and say 'tara' to mum. Then, just up the road and round the corner, I'd jump off the cart and go fishing with my dog Kim off the concrete blocks. I told my sister Freda not to let on she had a brother. I got away with that for six months or so. Some of the army lads knew what I was up to but never let on. In fact, I used to go to the canteen and play cards, dominoes and table tennis with them and help them eat their rations of sweets.

My dad's mother came through to see us and I took her to see my dad on the searchlight battery when a German plane flew right over us and machine gunned the lane we were walking down. My gran and I jumped into a ditch. I got there first and gran fell on top of me. She was all of twenty stone. I thought the aeroplane had fallen on me.

At the *Crown and Cushion*, the bar was our dining room but when it got to opening time, my sister and I were not allowed in. Dad had a butcher working with him. As I remember, we heard squealing one night and before morning there were sides of bacon and all that goes with it. When dad went home on leave, he was twice as fat as normal with a side of bacon wrapped round him under his topcoat.

Later, we went back to York. By now, our house had been made safe and just about habitable. There was just the *Cygnet* pub left and the outside shell of some of the houses – the crater had filled with water. Our gang made a camp out of rubble and old shattered timbers. I remember one day we were in camp having some tinned food we got out of one or two of the pantries and we were having a good old picnic when a Home Guard came in with a rifle and pointed it at us. He said: 'Do you know you can be shot for looting in wartime?' Well, you can imagine, we never went into a pantry again.

I remember granddad had two garden allotments on Scarcroft Stray. On a Thursday morning, cattle would arrive at Holgate railway yards for sale at York Cattle Market. I had to go with granddad's wheelbarrow and fill it up with cow manure and take it to the allotments before school. It was about three miles round journey. That wasn't bad but all my friends and the girls from the school saw me and called me names. You can imagine the smell but that's what we did for the war effort – Dig for Victory.

I did a lot of cinema going. At the Odeon, I would go in and make sure there were plenty of seats. If there were, I'd go to the toilets and lift the safety bar on the fire door and let my mates in. We tried it at the St Georges's Hall only once. We had to go round the back of the screen but our silhouettes were on for all to see. We got thrown out and told never to go back in.”

*28/29 April 1942.

Name: Ian Wright
Born: 1929
Wartime location: Cottingham

“I was ten years old in September 1939 and my brother was eight. We lived in Carisbrooke Avenue, Cottingham in 1939 and I remember listening to Prime Minister Chamberlain's broadcast then going out to find the streets deserted.

We boys were sent to Beverley Grammar School. We travelled by bus. Some vehicles towed gas-producer trailers, which frequently supplied insufficient fuel on the hills, causing the conductresses to walk behind poking the fire until it bucked up a bit!

Cottingham quickly became a temporary home to a succession of military units. Two groups of visitors were particularly noticeable for obvious reasons. One morning, we were surprised to notice that the house next door had been taken over by French Algerian troops in red fez's – all seemingly under five feet tall and perpetually smiling. Conventional French troops occupied Thwaite Hall for a period – and left some embarrassing graffiti and Cottingham played host for a short time to General Le Clerc and his tanks awaiting transport to Europe. The Americans when they arrived turned out to be coloured 'pioneer' soldiers all 'six-feet twelve' in height with commensurate girth, all dressed in immaculate uniforms and generous with their favours to us children and to the young ladies of the village. At that time, US coloured soldiers were not allowed to carry arms; officers and their military police were all white. As a sideline, dad made a fortune out of the Americans by charging them 2/6d to dance at the King Street Room to the Sylvena Dance Band, (geriatric but lively as I remember) packing the dancers in to the point of suffocation. Dad sat just inside the door, in what little fresh air there was, with his hat and coat on and a Gold Flake in his mouth, often accompanied by a local policeman bored with patrolling in the blackout. Incidentally, we discovered that the Yanks got 3/6d whenever the sirens sounded.

Cottingham, because of its proximity to Hull, had 824 alerts and Hull suffered 82 actual bombing raids, with Cottingham fortunately experiencing only the odd stray high explosive bomb with two near misses of parachute mines and a scattering of incendiaries. [For its size, Hull was the most bombed city in the UK.]

We boys harvested and swopped a rich collection of shell splinters, green parachute cord from the mines and occasional incendiary bombs, the latter carefully avoided later when we learned that the Germans had added delayed explosive charges to discourage tampering. When we were a little older, we made a few bike expeditions to the chalk pits at the top of Harland Rise, which were used as a temporary dump for unexploded bombs. There were usually about twenty in the eastern pit and we amused ourselves by sitting on them and trying to light some of the yellow contents which we scraped out with penknives then carried by all boys; perhaps just as well for us the explosives didn't burn very well! ”

Name: Don Booker
Born: Unknown
Wartime location: Barnsley

“The early years of war gave me my first experience of being a semi-professional musician, I was nine at the time and had a drum kit bought by my parents one Christmas. My school was in Burton Road, Old Mill where Geoff Haigh also attended. With men leaving to join the forces, there was a local shortage of musicians. We were the Geoff Haigh Dance Band, the only one in Britain still wearing short trousers!

Village halls and schoolrooms were the usual venues. Those weekly dances costing around 1s 6d were wonderful. They were the days of pink bras and suspender belts for those able to find stockings on the black market.

Coming from a brass band family, I turned to trumpet. The first band to include me as a trumpet player was at Barnsley Junior Technical College. Then a long spell with the Rhythm Swingtette started. The leader, the late Harry Swift (piano) made brilliant arrangements of big band numbers and I remember playing 'A String of Pearls' due to requests from Canadian soldiers who were camped at Cawthorne. Ma and Pa Brown would serve national cocoa, potted meat sandwiches and Quaker Oat crunch in the intervals.

Travel was always a problem with so much equipment and at one time, we went in an ice cream van until the owner was stopped by the police and told it was illegal. We then turned to a lorry. This provided plenty of cover with its high sides and no one knew we were inside.

We played at hundreds of dances free of charge for charities, prisoners of war and for injured miners at Pinderfields Hospital, Wakefield. All night dances were very popular too. I never made the top, as far as bands go, but those musical years did help the war pass quickly for a teenager. Being a member of a band gave one something to live for. ❞

(Don Booker was the former editor of the *Barnsley Chronicle*. This is an edited digest of an article that appeared in a special supplement of the *Barnsley Chronicle*: *Barnsley at War* published on 1 September 1989)

Name: Rita Millington
Born: 8 November 1929
Wartime location: Woodseats House Road, Sheffield

❝The war had only been declared two days earlier but when the sirens went, we were made to go in the shelter, mum insisting that we wear our gas masks. There we all were, struggling to breathe, as gas masks weren't the most comfortable of things. Our neighbours looked in on us when they returned to the house and nearly collapsed with laughing at the sight that greeted them – four people nearly choked to death. And it was only a practice!

Another time, Beryl and I climbed into the shelter and got wetter and wetter. Unbeknown to us, dad had struck a land drain and we were wet through and had to sit there shivering. Mum decided that we had better go back into the house as we could catch something sitting in wet clothes. We decided it was safer in the house. Dad made us a bed in the front room with a reinforced top on it. We had a door in our cellar, which was knocked through into next door's house as a way to escape if we were trapped with debris and not able to get out.

I can remember the night raids and hearing the planes overhead. The city centre was badly hit and I wasn't able to go to school as it meant lots of travelling and the tram track wasn't there. We went to a house in Chantry Road and used their front room as a classroom. We were taught by one of our teachers. I spent a few months in hospital during the early war years; a nurse sat by us during air raids. During one raid, the Germans dropped a huge bomb in Barkers Field. Dad took us to see the crater it made. How daft can you get? There were some unexploded bombs still around the area.

We used to have meat for dinner one day and the gravy the following day. Lots of vegetables were put in the pan with it and we had pavement slabs (chunks of bread) for dunking. One of the supposed teatime treats was thick slices of bread smeared with margarine – it was like hard lard – dipped in our ration of sugar. Sweets were almost non-existent. I can remember trying to make some mints with dried milk and peppermint essence. We thought they were good but today we wouldn't even attempt to eat them. Fresh fruit was not available at all but mum managed to obtain a banana. She took it to work and raffled it off and sent the money to Mrs Churchill for her Red Cross 'Aid to Russia' Fund. The Prime Minister's wife thanked me in a letter, which I still have.

For holidays, we went into Derbyshire on a farm. We had a bell tent and we helped the farmer in the fields with the planting and the harvest. It was very enjoyable away from the city. We never got any air raid sirens out in Derbyshire.

Mum worked at Laycocks Engineers making munitions; not a very nice job for females but they had to do it. Dad worked at Cravens Darnell. He was a carpenter by trade. He worked on parts for aircraft and trains.”

Name: Hilary B. Blackburne
Born: 1929
Wartime location: Anlaby Common, Hull

“Children in their hundreds were being evacuated to safe places in the countryside hopefully out of the way of German bombers. My parents decided to keep me at home to take my chances with them – they held the view that if a bomb had our name on it, at least we would all go together. Sometimes I'd venture outside to look for German aircraft caught in the searchlights and watch the anti-aircraft shells bursting all round causing planes to dip and dive. They used to drop flares to light up their targets – I used to think they looked very pretty – just like Bonfire Night! The landlord of the *Anlaby Park Hotel* made a promise to the anti-aircraft crews that he would give them a free barrel of beer for every German plane they managed to shoot down!

My father sent me to St Mary's Convent High School for Girls run by the Sisters of Mercy on Anlaby Road. I'd only been at the school a short time when we were told one morning that three girls from the school had been killed the night before in an air raid. We prayed for them. Not much longer after that the convent was gutted by incendiary bombs and the following morning I made up my mind to catch a bus and see if I could retrieve my school books which dad had had to work very hard to pay for. When I arrived, the fire service was still damping down the flames. There were fire hoses everywhere and a nun was walking up and down the lane saying her rosary. Then I spotted a girl I knew and together we decided to creep round to the back of the building which didn't appear to be too badly damaged to try and reach our classroom. We waded ankle-deep in water and broken glass trying to dodge charred beams which hung crazily from the ceiling. I finally found my desk and removed the books, dropping my biology book in the water so that the back peeled off. But the rest of them were in quite good shape. We never realised fully the danger we were in but, mercifully, we got in and out again completely unscathed.

I met a girl called Anita Valerie Gray who was a talented ballet dancer. We worked on a little act together, she doing a Polish dance while I accompanied her on the accordion. One day we heard that there was to be a grand concert in aid of Wings for Victory Week. Several local artistes were to appear and although nobody had ever heard of two fourteen year olds called Anita and Hilary we were both determined that they should do so. There we were doing our stuff before a packed audience. It was to prove an eventful evening for me as I was heard by someone connected with the Voluntary Entertainment Services concert parties which operated from Hull, entertaining at anti-aircraft and searchlight units situated on the banks of the Humber in such remote areas as Stone Creek and Sunk Island and also at RAF bomber Command at both Leconfield and Driffield. The units were very basic structures and more often than not the stage would be constructed from up-turned beer crates and many of the keys on the piano wouldn't play as a result of having beer poured onto them. The audience sat on wooden forms and after the show we would be treated to a cup of NAAFI tea and a rock bun. But the night that stands out most vividly in my memory was when we visited RAF Bomber Command at Leconfield.

In comparison with the army units, I can only describe Leconfield as luxurious. We were greeted by an officer who asked what we would like to drink. All the spirits that had long since disappeared from the shops were there – whisky, gin, rum, brandy – and I'll never forget the faces of the adult members of the party as they sipped the precious elixir. I, being the baby of the party, was only allowed a glass of orange juice! The large room where we were to give the concert was sumptuously furnished with red velvet drapes, carpeting and red leather armchairs. There was a bar at one side of the room and vases of chrysanthemums on small tables. We started the show with a few off-duty personnel lounging in the armchairs. About halfway through our routine, things started to happen. Our audience quickly disappeared one by one and, not knowing what was happening, we stopped the show. An officer appeared and tactfully recommended we finish the evening at a dance which was in progress in the NAAFI. Just then, the double doors at the end of the room opened and an entire bomb crew, who had just returned from a raid over Germany, entered still wearing their thick sheepskin flying jackets and boots. One by one they made their way to the bar, their faces white with anxiety and fatigue. I watched in amazement as they consumed one short after another until, almost collapsing into the red leather armchairs, they found their release in sleep.”

Name: Anne E. Dugdale
Born: 14 September 1936
Wartime location: Kenilworth Avenue, Hull

“It was an unnatural childhood. For the most part, I had only the lovely toys from before the war – a doll's pram, which was a replica of the Marmot pram in which my mother pushed me about, a replica doll's cot made in wood and two or three dolls dressed in their knitted outfits. I was given smaller things like balls and a skipping rope and a nurse's outfit during the war. Because of paper shortages and the high cost of books, I only had half a dozen or so books. We were taught to treasure and care for our possessions.

I was fortunate in having a holiday in the countryside each year with my mother and my friends, while my father stayed at home, afraid to leave our house in case of bomb damage. Our holidays were taken at the *Fox and Rabbit Inn* at Lockton, which was a pub and a farm serving full cream milk and honey from the comb; or we went to a wooden bungalow at Reighton. We had the beach to ourselves except when, occasionally, we saw a small group of soldiers relaxing in their off duty period; we were not allowed to speak to them.

We children were protected from the trauma as much as possible. There was a period though when I was put to bed in the Anderson shelter at the bottom of the garden; there was electric light and an electric fire and there were emergency rations of food and drink and first aid. My father had made three bunk beds for us; mine had to be extended as I grew taller. My mother had made siren suits for herself and me, warm all-in-one suits which were quick and easy to put on. There was a blast wall close to the entrance, but the shelter did not have a door. Instead, it had, what appeared to be an animal skin, stretched tightly across the entrance, so tightly that I was virtually imprisoned one Saturday morning when I had been left to sleep on after my parents had got up and gone to the house for breakfast.

In the school holidays, I was taken shopping in the town and I remember the devastation caused to so many buildings in the centre of Hull. I do remember Prospect Street and King Edward Street being non-existent on the infirmary side, except for the *Silver Grill Café*, which stood alone and isolated. All the shops had gone but I was fascinated by the fact that what had once been the marble and mosaic doorways and doorsteps still remained!

I remember saving waste during the war. We learned not to waste the end of the soap tablet, to save and reuse paper bags, to save string and to use every last bit of toothpaste in the tube. Baths were taken only once a week and when not in use, the bath was filled with water in case the house was hit by an incendiary bomb. And there were no streetlights. I remember men coming round after the war to prepare the street lights again. Unfortunately, birds had nested in many of them and their nests and nestlings were callously flung to the ground; my friend tried to rescue some of the baby birds but they were too young and frail to survive without their parents. ”

Name: Sheila Smith
Born: 1937
Wartime location: Wholesea Farm, Holme-on-Spalding Moor

“I was only two years old when the war broke out and it seemed natural to share our farmhouse with POWs. Karl Schmidt and Paul Hackenburg lived in as part of the family and worked every day on the farm. They had their own sitting room and slept there but we shared everything else. They ate what we ate and enjoyed our beef and Yorkshire puddings. They even babysat for my parents! They used to make us toys all from wood and I can remember a dolls house, a scooter and an acrobatic toy as well. They went back to the Storwood camp once a month and brought us things that were rationed and hard to get like soap. Paul had five children of his own and I suppose we little ones were part of his family.

Both men were good at making something out of nothing and if we wanted any repairs doing, they'd just go out and chop down a tree and make a new door or whatever was required.

Years after the war when my mother was dying, Karl came to see her as he felt that my parents were like a mother and father to him. And we still keep in touch.

There were lots of other POWs including some Italians working around Holme. One German got a job as a cowman at Hall Farm that belonged to the convent near the village and he married a local girl and started a milk round. I married my neighbour Ernest and we've been together for over fifty years! ”

Name: Wendy Pycock
Born: 21 March 1936
Wartime location: Hessle, Hull

“Every week at the Hessle C. of E. School, all the time I was in the infants, we had gas mask practice. Everyone was supposed to carry their masks at all times. I was so keen on mine that I sometimes wore it in bed. It was kept in a cream canister with a lid and a khaki webbing shoulder strap. I scratched my name on the circular tin base and decorated it with some scraps I'd swapped in exchange for several cigarette cards. Dad riveted luminous discs to the tin sides. They glowed sulphur yellow in the dark and could be worn on coat lapels. Dad said they were to avoid bumping into people. How dark it was in the streets in the winter months when there was no moon. The gas lamps stood unlit and houses loomed behind heavy blackout curtains. A chink of light was enough to bring the air raid warden hammering on the door with: 'Put that light out!'

My gas mask tin was easily identifiable in the school cloakroom. It was an adult model. I never qualified for a 'Mickey Mouse' type designed especially for kids. They were a bit soppy but the adult type meant one thing. I had a big head! And I had plaits.

One day I was off to town with mum. I went to my room to put on a clean dress, socks and best sandals. Gazing in the mirror I viewed the plaits still pinned up and I spied my gas mask under the stairs. Adjusting the straps, I plonked the mask over ribbons and plaits and studied the effect through the celluloid visor. I quite liked it. Still finding another last minute job to do, mum called: 'Go the front and watch for the bus.'

The bus was coming and so was mum. Without looking at me, she ran down the path, grabbed my hand and stepped on the bus. I slid into a seat by the window and mum followed. She still hadn't noticed my headgear. 'I think we'll go to Thornton's first' she said, turning to me as she spoke. 'What on earth! She exploded gazing at the snout of my gas mask. 'Is she expecting an air raid?' said the conductor. 'I don't know what she's expecting, but I know what she'll get if she doesn't take the damned thing off.' Thrusting her basket on my knee, mum hissed: 'Put it in there and stop being so ridiculous.'

Once off the bus, we headed for Hammonds, my plaits now in complete disarray. Mum retied my plaits. I looked at her in a mirror as she deftly plaited away, her lips remaining pursed as she gave the taffeta bows a final tug. 'Wait till we get home and I tell your father about your antics' she warned. 'And no more funny business my girl, or it'll be straight to bed and no tea for the rest of the week.' 'Blimey', I muttered, it's still only Monday.' ❞

(Included with the kind permission of the author, this entry is an abridged version of an article that appeared in issue No. 93 of *Down Your Way* magazine in August 2005.)

Name: Gladys E. Beadle
Born: Not Known
Wartime location: Keyingham

❝One night in June 1940 after school, my sister and I went to watch father haymaking in the field at Keyingham. He was sitting on the hay rake drawn by a white horse. Without any warning, a German plane dived and starting machine-gunning us. Father shouted, telling us to run to the edge of the field to lie down in the ditch. We were absolutely terrified but we ran as quickly as we could and lay down. Luckily, the ditch was dry but we were astounded to find lots of silver foil in the ditch, which we had been forewarned, could be contaminated. Meantime, father had taken his horse to shelter behind a big hedge. The plane few menacingly round and started machine-gunning again. Fortunately, it eventually flew away and we all went home safely.

In May 1941, there had been a very bad raid on Hull. We had been up most of the night. However, mother insisted that my sister and I try to get to our schools in Hull. There were only coaches running that morning – no double decker buses. We got as far as Hedon Road just past Saltend and met with a horrific sight. Both sides of the road, which were lined with timber yards, were ablaze. As we progressed, there were signs saying 'DIVERSION – UNEXPLODED BOMBS'. There were hose lines across the road in every direction. Eventually, after many diversions, my sister got off the bus and walked to school. I carried on, the bus taking many detours in and out of Holderness Road. It was a terrible sight – houses with all the bedrooms hanging out, shops and pubs in ruins and fires still burning. Also, there was this awful stench. There were women and children everywhere gathering up what they could salvage in their prams, homeless and distraught. Sad to say, all our efforts were in vain as both our schools were closed. ”

... EVACUEES

With the dawn of the aeronautical age exemplified by the exploits of pioneering aviators like Charles Lindbergh, Amelia Earhart and Yorkshire's own heroine Amy Johnson, the mass bombing of centres of industrial production became a real possibility, the limited experience of air raids during World War I when missions by Zeppelins and heavy bombers accounted for 1,400 fatalities further causing the authorities to expect the worst. Plans for the evacuation of mothers and children were made as early as 1934. In July 1939, the government issued a leaflet entitled *Evacuation – Why and How* to every household in the country, the leaflet identifying the Yorkshire cities of Sheffield, Leeds, Bradford, Hull (Middlesbrough was included later) as bomb vulnerable. The mass exodus to rural towns and villages was underway, tens of thousands of children leaving their parents on trips into the unknown.

On 1 September 1939, an astonishing 40,000 children left Leeds by rail in under seven hours and 6000 children were eventually relocated from Middlesbrough to Scarborough. Yorkshire's premier resort also experienced an influx of evacuees from Hull, amazed pupils finding themselves billeted alongside paying guests in prestige hotels like the *Adelphi*, the *Windsor*, the *Holbeck*, the *Astoria* and the elegant *Prince of Wales* where some quick-witted boys began to enjoy the high life, soon realising that if they left their shoes outside their bedroom doors at night, they became miraculously clean! Other children descended on the resorts boarding houses, one unhappy landlady complaining to the billeting officer: 'Please remove the two boys in my care. We came here to retire in peace and quiet and now this blight has come.'

Holiday haunts and sleepy rural towns and villages all across the county received their quotes of evacuees, one contingent of bewildered children leaving Gateshead for the wilds of the Yorkshire Dales, There, in the hamlet of Bainbridge, one boy and his sister found themselves billeted on a cruel Squeers – like farmer who beat his charges with a belt if they failed to work hard. Word filtered back to Gateshead and two aunts arrived 'as mad as hell and bundled us out of there.' The children were removed from Bainbridge to the mining village of Houghton in South Yorkshire where they received better treatment.

Posters were displayed in schools giving details of evacuation plans. The younger children had to have their names written on labels sewn onto their clothing and had to be presented at departure points carrying only the prescriptive one suitcase and a single allowable toy. Within fourteen hours of the evacuation order being given, the Women's Voluntary Service had recruited 120,000 women nationwide to assist in the task, one government official describing the mass movements as: 'An exodus bigger than that of Moses. It is the movement of ten armies, each of which is as big as the whole Expeditionary Force.' Lulled into a false sense of security by the lack of coordinated attacks by the enemy, almost 900,000 of the evacuated children were sent back home by 8 January 1940. Ironically, when the renewed threat of invasion peaked in May 1940, the whole process was reversed, thousands of children packing their bags for the second time.

Children, it had to be said, received a mixed reception, the derogatory term 'bloody vackees' describing some city urchins who arrived lousy with head lice, scabies and ringworm, others wetting their beds, snatching at food and eating with their fingers, stealing property, causing vandalism and using foul and abusive language. One foster mum expressed the ire of many in a fulsome letter to *The Spectator* magazine. 'Apart from the disgraceful insistence of the billeting people in thrusting filthy women and children into the homes of decent, cleanly people, there is the economic hardship not yet mentioned. Many of the evacuated children arrived with no change of various undergarments. This means that the struggling country worker's wife must buy new socks and vests for the slum children or allow them to become even more malodorous than they already are.' Some children received frosty receptions and hated leaving home. For some little mites though, it was a revelation and an end to sleeping under their parents' beds and dozens of other privations, including the expedient of having to be sewn into their underwear, which, in some cases, was only changed in spring and autumn. In that first year of evacuation, the winter was very severe with heavy snowfalls. During the freeze, hot water bottles became prize possessions, some youngsters using the tepid water in their bottles to wash before breakfast.

Householders who took displaced children received 10s 6d per week for the first child and 8s 6d for subsequent children. Parents had to contribute to the costs of maintaining their children. Costs were waived for the poorest families but were means tested. Ninety percent of children went to private households; 10 per cent were directed to purpose-built camps. Some householders were choosy, prodding and poking and examining parted scalps for head lice, scenes 'reminiscent of a cross between a Roman slave market and Selfridges bargain basement' ensuing. The modern film *Goodnight Mister Tom* starring the late John Thaw is an accurate reflection of the conditions and attitudes at the time.

Some evacuees so enjoyed the experiences of relocation that they stayed in their adoptive home towns and villages to bring up families of their own. Others hated the whole thing, one city woman complaining: 'I'm going home. I'd rather be bombed on my own doorstep than stay here and die of depression.'

One of the most eccentric but loveable Yorkshire couples to act as adopted parents were Mr and Mrs Chew from Burniston, near Scarborough. The larger than life Mr Chew was the village blacksmith who had the habit of wearing one of his wife's cardigans wrapped tightly round his waist. Mrs Chew had a similarly breezy character rejoicing in painting her village cottage in the brightest of colours. Five evacuees, who all returned with nostalgia to their wartime billet, recall the lady tying a rope to her brass bedstead and around her waist and abseiling down the front of her home with a red paint pot.

Some evacuees were shipped abroad to countries far away from the conflict. In 1940, 480 British children were evacuated on the Polish ocean liner MV *Batory*, a legendary vessel known as the *Lucky Ship*. She was initially bound for Cape Town in South Africa. Such, however, was the developing rapport and friendship between the children and the Polish crew that the Admiralty gave permission for the ship to sail on to Australia where the children were landed in Fremantle, Melbourne and Sydney. The epic 20,000 miles voyage was completed in just seventy-two days enlivened by constant partying and singing, in three subsequent books about her adventures, *M/V Batory* also being dubbed the *'Singing Ship'*.

Name: Katherine Parkin
Born: Not known
Wartime location: Barnsley

“The steam train wearily drew its last gasp as it pulled into Barnsley railway station. It was the end of a gruelling nine-hour journey for us – my mother, sisters and myself. The journey had been interrupted several times. Wearily, we had been forced to alight from the train due to bombing raids on towns through which the train had travelled on its way from London. We got out of the train in Barnsley to a scene of pitch-blackness and grime – and what on earth were people talking about? It could have been the moon on which we had landed. Everyone was speaking a foreign language or so it seemed.

To begin with, we couldn't come to terms with the quietness. No sound of throbbing aircraft. No sound of falling buildings and the breaking of glass. No craters in the ground and demolished houses, shops and churches. But Barnsley was our saviour and we shall always be thankful for that.”

(This is an edited extract from an article that appeared in a special supplement of the *Barnsley Chronicle*: *Barnsley at War* published on 1 September 1989)

Name: Beaty Coulman
Born: 1934
Wartime location: Bishop Wilton

‘‘I was evacuated on a bus. The local children all stood round looking at us. I remember them looking very pretty in little bonnets, dressed entirely different from us. I went up the hill to Mrs Stead's. The picture is so vivid; it was the biggest back kitchen you've ever seen with flagstones. Turkeys used to walk in and out while we were eating. We all had to have our hair cut because they said that the evacuees had brought head lice. I can't remember being distressed. I can't remember crying.

The walnut tree was double and we could reach it out of the bedroom window and we used to eat the walnuts in bed. I'd eat them until I was sick. I still don't eat walnuts.

The two girls I was with were a lot older than me. I can remember them putting me in the beck and throwing me in a bunch of nettles. For a laugh. I don't think it was serious.

I remember going to Butcher Smith's and in the outbuildings we tried to make elderberry wine. We used to get jam jars and squash elderberries into them and leave them on the beams thinking that the next day they'd be elderberry wine. But the next day, it'd be all-fusty on top. Auntie kept a pig in the back and it'd get slaughtered and they used to hang it all up on the beams to cure it. Anyone that had a pig slaughtered that day would bring you a pig fry and a bucket of blood to make the black pudding with. What I wouldn't give for a bit of that black pudding! It was gorgeous when you got home on a dinner time.

We had to work hard. I can remember if Renee didn't dust properly between the spells on the back of the chair, auntie would draw ‘Renee’ in the dust. And you weren't allowed to shout ‘Hiya!’ in the village like a greeting. You had to say ‘Hallo’ properly. We had good teaching. We were taught table manners. We had to stand at table to eat – we weren't allowed to sit. I always say we were fortunate in that we didn't know what it was like to be hungry; we ate well. I don't think that people in the country were aware of what war meant at all. They were amazed when the flour went dark. There may have been shortages but they bottled things, made jam and put eggs down. Auntie Annie had a big terracotta pot with isinglass in for preserving the eggs. They bottled all their vegetables. And they always had a big baking day every Thursday and baked lots of pies that lasted all week. And we used to go down Bolton Lane to gather rosehips because there was a drive for rosehip syrup. It was an organised thing. We had baskets from school to do it properly.

One of the things I remember most is the Home Guard. It was proper Dad's Army. I'm sure they thought that the Germans were going to march into Bishop Wilton and shoot us all down.

We went up the hills on Easter Monday to roll eggs after colouring them. We used to boil them with cochineal and then draw faces on them. We'd roll them to see who's lasted longest without cracking.

I remember going to the pictures to get your present off the Americans. I always remember that because I got a box of paints off the Yanks that big I couldn't carry it home on the bus. The villagers were upset because only the evacuees got a present. And once they came and measured us up for clothes and shoes and when it came to my feet they said: 'What size shoes do you take?' and I said 'Elevens in the week and twelve's on Sundays.' Of course, my best shoes were twelve's.

And we went potato picking. You got 5 shillings a week for it. The worst thing about the tatie picking was that after you'd picked all the taties, they ploughed it all up again and you had to pick all the bits up for the pigs.

We had earth toilets. We used to have to put ash on top. If you went up to the toilet when Mr West was on, you had to shut the door and come back out again because you didn't want to be sat next to Mr West! We had bits of newspaper on a nail – we strung them together. What I often did as well was to cut rags for clipped rugs.

Our mums couldn't get to Bishop Wilton because there was no petrol. McMasters ran a bus from Hull in the summer for six weeks and then they'd come and see us. And my mother used to go in the pub. I bet they thought she was real common. ”

These recollections were first recorded by Mike and Kate Pratt for an evacuee's anniversary event held in Bishop Wilton and I'm grateful to them for permission to quote from their transcript which concludes:

“Beaty left Bishop Wilton when she was nine and is left with two good lessons. She remembers going out when it was snowing to sledge down the bank. On returning and saying 'I'm cold', she got the response, 'you aren't cold, you only think you are.' She's never been cold since. Also when it was dark and the village was blacked out and the others were frightened, Beaty volunteered to go to the fish shop. She's never been frightened of the dark since. ”

On 10 October 1941, the *Hull Daily Mail* published the following (edited) article about the evacuation of children to Bishop Wilton:

❝It is an undiluted joy to record that one party of Hull children have stayed in one place for two years without a single member making treks for home. It speaks volumes for the parents who have sacrificed their affection for the safety of their children, and the spirit of understanding and generosity of the villagers who have undertaken this very humane task of looking after our men and women of the future.

There are fifty-four children between the ages of four and thirteen years evacuated to Bishop Wilton all of whom come from the Holderness Road, Hull. The children are as happy as possible and share all their activities with the village children and there have been no serious complaints, although when they first arrived there was some misunderstanding among the tiny ones about the ownership of apples growing on trees. But they have responded magnificently to kindness and there has been no further bother of any kind.❞

Name: Diana H. Harrison
Born: 3 April 1925
Wartime location: Westtown School, Pennsylvania, USA and Brackley, Northamptonshire

❝I was born at 44 Park Drive, Heaton, Bradford. We relocated several times, finally moving to Brackley in Northamptonshire so my memories of Bradford are vague. I do remember, though, going to Rossfield Kindergarten School in Heaton. I also recall my grandparent's house in Clifton Villas and going to the market in Manningham Park. My mother used to take me to Brown Muff's department store. I was allowed to have hot chocolate.

In April 1940, I decided to go to the US to stay with friends of my father's. Originally the scheme to evacuate children to the US was sponsored by the Boston Transcript newspaper. It went bankrupt just prior to my departure so my father paid.

When the time came, I felt numb. The trip to London that October to meet the group at Grosvenor House was eerie and grey. London had been bombed and seemed shocked. We had an American woman escort for six or eight children. She took us to Liverpool during an air raid. We spent two days awaiting embarkation in Liverpool air raid shelters before boarding three Cunard ships. Two of them I recall were named *Samaria* and *Sophia*. They left under an RAF escort for the first 100 miles. We took two weeks to reach New York on a zigzag course.

We spent the first night at the Seamen's Institute (no seamen there!). The next night I was put on the Lehigh Valley Railroad to Ithaca. I was met by new foster parents Paul and Christine. Paul was my father's roommate at Oxford after the First World War. I had never met them before. They were very good to me. They sent me to a Quaker co-ed boarding school in Pennsylvania. It was founded in 1799.

My mother wrote to me every week with news of my family. I knew food was scarce. But they were lucky. They had six hens in the back garden. Brackley was pretty rural in those days.

I had 2½ years in the US, returning to the UK in June 1943 in a big convoy of eighty-eight ships from New York. I was on the *Johann de Witt*, which had been taken over by the British Navy. It was packed with US troops and hundreds of civilians. We landed at Southampton. I took several trains to get home to Brackley and had a great reunion with my parents. My brother was away in the navy serving as a radar operator on HMS *Redpole*. Rationing was severe when I went back. Shortages of fat and sugar were very noticeable. The bread was a dirty white colour but it tasted ok.

Yorkshire was always important to me. I used to go to Wensleydale to stay with my aunt who had a cottage in Newbiggin just up the hill from Askrigg. My family came from Yorkshire so it was in our blood. My mother and her sister bought a house in Masham. We had many happy times there. I have always loved the Dales. When my future husband came to visit me in August 1946, I took him to Wensleydale. We rode old bicycles all the way to Bolton Castle and Leyburn! So little traffic on the roads then; it was marvellous! ❞

Diana eventually married and settled in the US, writing to me recently from her Haverford home. In her letter, she recalls her exceptional father-in-law:

❝My father-in-law was a wonderfully warm person. He was always very good to me. He worked very hard so we didn't see much of him. When he did have spare time, he loved working on his garden. ❞

Diana's daughter Diana Comber has since explained why her grandfather had such little free time. In 1945, Earl G. Harrison, the Dean of Penn Law School was sent by President Truman to investigate the plight of displaced persons in Europe. With an end to the hostilities, he visited thirty camps expecting improvements but he recoiled at the appalling conditions still endured by Jewish Holocaust survivors and others. He found widespread malnutrition, serious overcrowding and unhygienic conditions, noting the continuing presence of barbed wire and, in one case, the sight of inmates living in horse stalls. According to eyewitness accounts, the envoy broke down in tears. Fired to action, he prepared one of the most incendiary reports in US legal history, dropping the bombshell on the President's desk and demanding action. Stinging and highly controversial he fulminated against the US military for 'treating the Jews as the Nazis treated them except that we do not exterminate them ... One has to wonder whether the German people, seeing this, are not supposing that we are following or at least condoning Nazi policy.' Within three weeks, Truman ordered European theatre commander Dwight D. Eisenhower to improve conditions in the camps, the entire report commanding national attention in an unexpurgated front-page publication by the *New York Times* on 30 September 1945. The ultimate responsibility for conditions in the camps lay with the swashbuckling but cantankerous old warhorse General George Patton and he was relieved of his command, new initiatives creating all Jewish camps, closing concentration camps and transferring refugee care to the United Nations Relief and Rehabilitation Administration.

Harry Reicher, Penn Law School adjunct professor and board member of the US Holocaust Memorial Museum suggests that in galvanising public opinion, the report provided the impetus for far reaching changes in immigration law that allowed several hundred thousand Jewish immigrants to enter the US. He also contends that it helped create a climate for the establishment of the State of Israel in 1948. By 1952, the US had welcomed 395,000 displaced persons.

The author's son, J. Barton Harrison, who established the Earl G. Harrison Human Rights Fund at Penn Law School in his father's memory said: 'He was always for the underdog and for those who were less fortunate. He didn't think that human beings should be treated that way.'

Name: John Crathern
Born: 14 April 1939
Wartime location: 1 Scott Cottages, Scott Hill, Clayton West

“I was born in Millwall just before the outbreak of World War Two. Shortly after hostilities commenced, it was decided by the government that because of German air raids, London was by now too dangerous a place for young children and that all children above the age of two should be evacuated to safer locations.

When my time came, I suppose I was taken to a London station to be put on a train to Yorkshire. I was probably carrying a small bag of possessions and most certainly a label explaining who I was and my destination. I don't actually remember the journey to Yorkshire but my first memories are of the happy times playing with my new found friends in and around the village of Clayton West. But I suppose there must have been some sort of Reception Committee to organise the children and unite them with their new foster parents.

The couple who became my foster parents were George and Ethel Bedford. George was a miner working at the local mine at Clayton West, although mining was a tough job in those days. I remember him as a kind and gentle person. I imagine that being a housewife during the war wasn't easy either, but Ethel was kindness itself. The Bedford's had grown up children of their own, two daughters (Minnie and Bessie) and a son, Dennis. It was very brave of them to take on a two-year-old boy with a funny accent at their time of life. Sadly, George was killed in a mining accident in 1942.

People ask: 'It must have been a traumatic experience being taken from your parents and sent to Yorkshire? I always answer: 'No. The trauma was being taken back to London at the end of the war.' You can imagine being taken from a lovely village in the Yorkshire countryside to the devastation of the East End of London. Clayton West had turned me into a country boy and I have remained so all my life. I found it very difficult to settle in London and was finally shipped off to my mother's parents who moved to Essex.

My memories of Clayton West are of a little village in the middle of the countryside where everybody knew all the other people. I wanted to return all through my adult life but never got around to doing so. Eventually, when I retired, my wife and I decided that we would leave it undone no longer, so we got down to planning.

Firstly, we thought we would contact the local post office and church with a view to displaying a plea to the local community for help in recognising people in a collection of photographs taken during my time there. Sometime later, we were absolutely astounded to receive a phone call from BBC Leeds asking if we would be prepared to broadcast our plea for help live on air. Apparently, a BBC producer was a customer of the local post office and noticed our plea for help. The broadcast took place a few days later, with me in the BBC studio in Swansea and linked to BBC Radio Leeds. The very next day, the *Yorkshire Evening Post* rang to ask that when I returned to Clayton West could they send a reporter and photographer to meet me and follow me round. So there I was at the age of sixty-seven going back for the first time. I have to admit to the odd butterfly or two in my stomach as the thoughts raced through my mind. The journey seemed to take forever and I became more and more nervous as we passed through Sheffield and Barnsley and then, quite suddenly, I was back. I needn't have worried. The village was still recognisable as the Clayton West where I spent those happy years.

After two wonderful days, we felt that we might not be able to discover any descendents of the Bedford's, so we reluctantly returned home to Swansea. A few days later, an article was published in the *Yorkshire Evening Post*. The response from readers was fantastic. Not only have we been able to put names to people in the photographs but we've been able to contact them. It's been so wonderful to speak to the grandchildren of the Bedford's and to a lady who, when she was a little girl, was also evacuated from Millwall to Clayton West and fostered by the Bedford's daughter Minnie. Her name was Jean Martin and she now lives in California with her husband Milo Cripps.

I feel as if I've been on a journey of discovery and finally reached my destination and feel a strong sense of completeness in my life. ”

... GENERAL PRACTITIONERS

Inspired by patriotic fervour like other professional men, many GPs enlisted for military service during the war, leaving their practices in the hands of older men like Will Pickles of Wensleydale who was a fifty-four-year-old veteran when hostilities were declared in 1939. In country districts like his and in cities and towns across Yorkshire, GPs were hard pressed, the lack of medicines and drugs, the injury and trauma of bombing and the constant fear of bombing, the high accident rates as a consequence of the blackout and the recruitment of unskilled labour into factories, the mass movement of populations which fuelled epidemics and the general assault on health resulting from long hours in the fields and factories, all doubling workloads. Some doctors took to drink, buckled under the strain and became as ill as their patients but one Yorkshireman became the most outstanding GP of his generation.

Name: William Norman Pickles
Born: 6 March 1885
Wartime location: West Burton and Aysgarth (surgery), Wensleydale
Will Pickles was born in Leeds and was educated at Leeds Grammar School. He studied medicine at the Yorkshire College and trained at the Leeds General Infirmary going on to become an assistant at a country practice in Bedale, his close observation of outbreaks of cholera among the itinerant gypsy population alerting him to the causes of epidemics. His first appointment in Aysgarth was as a locum to Dr Hime in 1912. Soon afterwards, he took a position as ship's doctor on a voyage to Calcutta, returning to England in the same year to a more permanent post as second assistant to Dr Hime. Collaborating with his first assistant colleague Dean Dunbar, an old student friend, he helped buy out the practice in 1913. After the First World War, when he served as a surgeon lieutenant with the Royal Naval Volunteers, he developed a reputation as an outstanding GP and a pioneering epidemiologist becoming famous and attracting a string of honours including an Honorary Doctorate of Science from Leeds University and the CBE.

Inspired by Sir James Mackenzie's *The Principles of Diagnosis and Treatment in Heart Affections,* Pickles investigated a 1929 epidemic of catarrhal jaundice, 250 people out of a Wensleydale population of 5,700 falling victim to the disease. Using extensive local knowledge and his considerable talents as a medical detective, he traced the outbreak to a girl who he had examined on the morning of a village fete, dedicated research establishing the incubation of the disease of between twenty-six and thirty-five days. An account of the epidemic was published in the *British Medical Journal*, similar articles about his experiences treating Sonne dysentery and Bornholm disease following in subsequent years. Pickles expounded his discoveries to the Royal Society in 1935, a subsequent leading article in the *British Medical Journal* suggesting: 'It may be the beginning of a new era in epidemiology'.

Pickles's ground-breaking book *Epidemiology in Country Practice* came out in the year war was declared in 1939. The book was published by John Wright in Bristol in May but all remaining stocks were destroyed in an air-raid in April 1941. Reprinted in 1949, it became a medical classic and a valued text book which is still in print today, demonstrating that country practices, far from being backwaters of medical knowledge and research, could be harnessed as unique field laboratories with unparalleled opportunities for epidemiological research.

From his surgery in Aysgarth and Town Ends, his bungalow home in the pretty village of West Burton where he lived from 1922 to 1952, Dr Pickles developed an outstanding practice, even the additional workloads imposed by the conflict of 1939–45 failing to sap his energy or inhibit his researches. With total dedication and an unfailing rapport with his 5,000 or so patients scattered in eight villages and isolated hamlets across Wensleydale, Dr Pickles became as affectionately synonymous with that part of rural Yorkshire as its cheese. His very presence uplifted the spirit, his warm and unassuming bedside manner and his uncanny knack for a quick diagnosis and treatment, acting as a one-man placebo effect over the entire dale. His patients loved him and he loved his dale and its hard working farming stock, his revolutionary ideas about the importance of underpinning medical assessments with an intimate knowledge of patients' lifestyles, of social conditions and empirical research examining historical events like the Wensleydale plague of 1563, gradually percolating wider practice. In one of his many lectures, he spoke of his impressions of his home:

“I remember a particularly lovely evening in early summer when I climbed to the top of Addleborough. The sun was setting and it lit up the grim pile of Bolton Castle. Lovely little Semerwater seemed to lie at my feet and one by one, I made out most of our grey villages with their thin palls of smoke. And as I watched the evening train creeping down the valley with its pauses at our three stations, a quaint thought came into my head and it was that there was hardly a man, woman or child of whom I did not know the Christian name and with whom I was not on terms of intimate friendship. My wife and I say that we know most of the dogs and indeed some of the cats. I am grateful to my very dear friends in Wensleydale. I would not have spent my life elsewhere for all the wealth of the Indies.”

For nine months early in the Second World War, Will and his wife Gerty were foster parents to two boy evacuees from Sunderland, the influx of extra mothers and children into the dale engendering lots of extra work especially as a consequence of the customary head lice and diarrhoea. Many of the inquisitive and unruly evacuees were unaccustomed to country ways and to farm life, their unfamiliarity with animals and machinery leading to a spate of accidents with further calls on the magic black bag. Some of these evacuees also reintroduced diphtheria although the disease was soon contained and, on the very first day of the mass arrivals, Will was summoned to deliver a visiting mother's twins. Wensleydale's wartime population was swelled even further by contingents of well-to-do people who fled the bomb vulnerable cities to take refuge in dales hotels such as the *Palmer Flatt* in Aysgarth. The conflict further imposed on Will and his practice partner's time, the patients of a Hawes doctor who was conscripted into the forces, joining their lists.

In 1940, a tragedy afflicted the dale that was totally unconnected with the war. The local Morris Grange TB sanatorium for children burnt down and its occupants were displaced, the doctor in charge telephoning Will to ask if he could help finding alternative accommodation. Will instantly recalled a conversation with his father-in-law Harry Tunstill, a wealthy Burnley mill owner who built Thornton Lodge near Thornton Rust in 1909 as a holiday home. 'Harry had once said to me: "It will make a very good sanatorium some day." I tackled my wife's mother at Thornton Rust who at eighty-six made up her mind instantly. "Of course the children can come to Thornton Lodge," she said realising all the implications. Two buses arrived with children, staff and an incredible amount of bedding and stores and all were somehow accommodated. Finally, the County Council bought the house at a very low figure and it became the Children's Sanatorium for the Riding.' Amazingly, Will still found time to develop his ideas on epidemiology and in 1942 he made application for the Milroy lectureship awarded annually by the Royal College of Physicians for delivery in London. His application was accepted but the lecture hall was bombed, Will having to resort to the publication of his *Epidemic Disease in English Village Life in Peace and War* in the *University of Leeds Medical School Magazine*. Despite the peripheral importance of that publication in *medical academia*, the treatise provoked national and subsequently international interest. His impressions about the medical impact of the evacuee programme made fascinating reading:

"In few respects has village life been altered by war conditions and in respect of epidemic disease there is little to tell. Village life has indeed been altered already in some ways. Householders, a few gladly and graciously, many with resignation and some with bitter resentment, had accepted small, town children as guests (hardly paying guests) into their houses, possibly to bring with them disease and even death to their own little sons and daughters. On the 15th September 1939, exactly a fortnight after the date of the first reception of evacuees, a little boy, a native child, fell ill with diphtheria and his brother became a victim four days later. These children, being newcomers to the village and actually unknown to me, had not received protective inoculation. An unfortunate chance had brought an evacuee to this of all houses and this child I was told had been suffering from a sore throat for a week. He was one of those to whom country life made no appeal and I never saw him as he went back to his home on 16th September, the day after his first victim was attacked and three days before the second. Impetigo, nits, scabies, enuresis struck terror in the hearts of the foster parents, but unfortunately in this instance a sore throat was regarded with indifference. One epidemic was most definitely introduced by an evacuee. Our district seems fated to suffer from jaundice epidemic. I here produce a chart showing as the first sufferer an evacuee girl, her train of victims being thirteen in all, including three evacuee boys. ”

In September 1942, the *Lancet* commented on the lecture paper with a certain begrudging and deprecating haughtiness. ‘These lectures breathe the spirit of the countryside and it is easy to visualise with the author the cheerful, high spirited bus-loads of country folk exchanging jokes and germs as they make their pilgrimages from the Wensleydale villages to market or to the cinema in the country towns.’

The *British Medical Journal* was a little more generous: ‘. . . his contributions to epidemiology are much like those of Gilbert White to natural history – jewels on a small scale, of value not for their rarity, but for their workmanship.’

By 1943, Will’s book had an international readership, an impressed John Gordon, Professor of Epidemiology at Harvard who was serving with the American forces in Europe, expressing a desire to meet its author. ‘Very well,’ said a Ministry of Health doctor in London, ‘we’ll invite him to London to meet you’.

‘No sir,’ answered Gordon, ‘I want to go and see him in this goddam little country town where he does his epidemiology.’ Gordon visited Aysgarth and stayed with the Pickles family at Town Ends. The two doctors had an animated discussion, Gordon praising Will’s work but pointing out a serious flaw in his researches in that the ages of all the patients Will had treated at the time of their illnesses had not been noted. After Gordon left with a lecture invitation to visit Harvard after the war, Will painstakingly amended his omission by analysing his records over the previous ten years.

Later on in the war, Will joined a number of prestigious local and national medical advisory bodies, furthering his researches into influenza (there was a serious outbreak in November 1943 at Askrigg Grammar School, the national death toll topping 1,000) rheumatic fever and rheumatic heart disease. 'In our influenza epidemic,' he later confided with typical humour, 'George Cockcroft (a colleague) ascended the stairs where an elderly husband and wife were in bed with the disease. He realised they were quarrelling, the old man having the last word as Cockcroft entered the room; "If thou was in t'churchyard, there'd be more room in this bed!"'

In 1944, Pickles was asked by the government to contribute to a study on birth control. He told the researchers that in Wensleydale, recourse to instrumental abortion was almost non-existent and that although the employment of abortifacients was rare, there was some use of the pennyroyal plant. He added that courting between engaged couples usually embraced sexual intercourse but '... local chemists say there is little demand for contraceptives.' Will brought much homespun wisdom to the inquiry commenting: 'These are just the people to keep a doctor in his investigations. Matters so delicate as consanguinity and heredity have to be approached with care, but on the whole, I have found my patients cooperative and slow to take offence.'

Also in 1944, Will delivered a lecture to the Yorkshire branch of the Society of Medical Officers, examining, amongst other topics, the condition known to afflict farmers who handled mouldy hay. Doctors, he opined, had been slow to recognise the causes of a disease that led to breathlessness and disability. He went on to describe the examination of an upland farmer who had difficulty breathing when hay was harvested in the rainy season, admitting: 'I can realise that if I had had that true humility and willingness to learn, this 'Farmer's Lung', as I think it should be called, would have been identified on not a few occasions and much suffering avoided.' His typically descriptive name for a disease that has since been largely eliminated by the extraction of dust from newly mown hay, has stuck to this day.

Throughout the war, Pickles was beset by problems, his popularity as a doctor ironically attracting more patients to his list. He worked tirelessly and with good cheer, a fellow GP, Dr J. A. Simpson, writing this: 'From what I can read between the lines, you seem to be reacting to all the wartime problems with your unfailing good humour and kindliness and even evacuation has not shaken your equanimity – nor your faith in the good outweighing the evil.'

Having lost a leg, Will Pickles died of pneumonia in 1963. His obituary in the *British Medical Journal* reads as follows:

“Will was a great family doctor, scrupulously careful in his recording and visiting, never underrating a patient or his symptoms. He was courteous and kind to all, even the most awkward patients.”

A Pickles memorial plaque was unveiled in Aysgarth in May 1971. The most heart-warming eulogy to his name is embodied in a Joan Pomfret poem, which ends:

They will remember evermore,
His name in Wensleydale.

Dr Pickles's biography, *Will Pickles of Wensleydale – The Life of a Country Doctor*, by John Pemberton, was published in 1970.

Will Pickles was the first President of the Royal College of General Practitioners, the college safeguarding a collection of his private papers including case notes, drafts of speeches and lectures and letters, these papers forming the basis of the entries above. In visiting the college and examining the Pickles Collection, I immediately warmed to the doctor's obviously kind personality and openness, epitomised by his flowing and very readable handwriting – not a typical physician! Jumping from the pages, the following additional extracts from some of his notes speak keenly of the man and of Wensleydale.

“Hime sent me to visit three old ladies in Aysgarth village whose ages added up to over 270 years. Not a bad place to settle in I thought. Shortly after this, Dunbar and I set out on horseback on Sunday afternoon to visit certain patients who lived in a remote side dale Walden and access to whom was only possible by that mode of transport. In one of the most remote of these, a farmer sat crouched over the fire. As we spoke to him, his thin shoulders were shaken by a dreadful cough and he spat frequently and some of his sputum did not reach the fire. The kitchen seemed to be filled with dark curly-headed little girls and we chased them away while we stripped their father for examination. The signs were only too obvious and as we took back his sputum in an old Bovril jar and late though was the hour of our return, stained and examined it. That man died at the age of eighty but three of those delightful children died in early womanhood from pulmonary tuberculosis. No one can blame that poor fellow. Even today the public is insufficiently informed of the infectiousness of this dread disease and probably all those little children were infected before we were called in.

I cannot describe adequately the delight that I experienced right from the beginning of my life here. I had quite definitely fallen on my feet in what I might describe as the practice of my dreams. At Aysgarth, I had congenial surroundings, a congenial partner, but as much as those, kindly, friendly, cooperative patients.

I should like to say much about the character of the people of the Yorkshire Dales ... I must acknowledge their intelligence and shrewdness which helped me in my investigations into epidemics on many occasions. The typical Dalesman or Daleswoman is deeply interested in illness, their own and more particularly other peoples and I have got much correct information from listening like Sir Walter Scott to the 'auld wife's tale' rather than by asking questions.

I could say much of the Yorkshire Dalesman and Daleswoman of their shrewdness and ability and of the seemingly impenetrable crust which is only a crust hiding great friendliness and goodness of heart. ”

In being presented face-to-face with his portrait – it is now given pride of place in the patrician splendour of the offices of the Royal College in Hyde Park London – Will commented: 'I don't look happy in it and I've always been happy.' The fact that he was immensely happy is revealed by a further reading of his lecture notes. Many of these are liberally sprinkled with such comical ginger as this:

“ William Winn bet a man a pint of beer he couldn't balance a penny on his forehead and drop it into a tin funnel fixed in his waistcoat. While he was balancing the penny, Winn poured the pint of beer down the funnel.

The same William Winn ordered a whisky and turned to the landlord saying: 'There's something wrong here, you've been watering it.' Handing it to William Wilkinson he said: 'You taste it', whereupon Wilkinson drank the lot and said he could taste 'nowt wrong wi' it.' ”

Renown as the greatest practical joker in the dale, this William Winn lived in Askrigg, regularly 'watering' at the *King's Arms*. In his notes, Will records the wags most famous caper, Winn plying an old man with copious drink and then betting him £5 that he couldn't undress in five minutes. The inebriated fellow swallowed the bait and clumsily undressed, standing naked in the bar in only his boots, the unyielding knots in his laces refusing to budge despite repeated tugs and strains as everything danced and dangled. 'Cut the wangs' (bootlaces) implored an impassioned Winn handing his victim a knife, the old man sawing away with trembling fingers and winning his bet with a triumphant cheer. Winn promptly paid his dues, writing out a makeshift cheque on a telegraph form. Finally, he threw the strippers clothes on a high shelf in the tap room and rang a loud bell to summon the bar maid.

(These notes have been compiled from papers incorporated in the Pickles Collection. I am indebted to the Royal College of General Practitioners who gave permission for me to freely quote from the collection.)

... NURSES

The vast majority of professional women during the war were employed either as teachers or nurses. By 1938, the nursing profession was 154,000 strong. They were all needed.

During the early stages of the 'Phoney War' hospital admissions increased, road traffic and other accidents caused by the universal blackout enforcements and additional mishaps in factories that began to employ workers unaccustomed to using dangerous machinery, providing a steady stream of patients. The shortage of soap and the exhortations about the economic use of bathwater led to a fall in personal hygiene standards, close confinement in homes and in air raid shelters exacerbating the problem to create infestations of lice and fleas, outbreaks of boils, impetigo and scabies all increasing the workload for hard pressed nurses. Once the shooting started, however, the clinics and wards were cleared to receive battle casualties and every bed was occupied by the chronically sick and injured, stately homes, castles and manor houses across the county being requisitioned as makeshift hospitals. The former home of famous naturalist and taxidermist Charles Waterton, Walton Hall, near Wakefield was typical of the many such properties pressed into service.

Hastily trained teenage ambulance workers waited at railway stations in their far from sophisticated vehicles. Poorly sprung and prone to the percolation of exhaust gases, they were equipped with two double metal bunks for four patients, only roll-up curtains at the back keeping out the weather. As trains arrived, often late at night, ambulance workers readied their stretchers and prepared hot water bottles and drinking flasks for each man, looking out for red crosses on the foreheads of those casualties whose tourniquets would require releasing every ten minutes to prevent gangrene setting in. Then it was off to hospital, taking care to avoid the ruts and bomb craters.

Hospitals like the Pinderfields Emergency unit in Wakefield were nearly entirely reserved for such war-wounded servicemen. In an attempt to minimise alarm, many of the patients arrived at Wakefield Station under the cover of darkness in specially adapted trains. Anonymous behind blacked-out windows, the casualties were cared for by the Red Cross. One nurse recalls the secrecy of the operations in 1944, remembering the sight of camouflaged lorries ferrying the patients to the awaiting night staff, the hospital cook always insisting on greeting the men with freshly cooked fish and chips.

Casualties could be transported from distant battlefields by train within eighteen hours of being wounded. Some of these were badly mutilated and dreadfully burnt, experienced nurses draping end-of-the-bed sheets and blankets over metal frames to dissipate the awful smells. 'When we opened the plaster, we found maggots eating the detritus but we just closed the plaster up again to let the maggots finish the good work.'

Across the county, nurses experienced such nightmarish horrors of war at first hand and they often had to work for forty-eight hours round the clock. One twenty-seven-year-old veteran was an operating theatre specialist responsible for preparing instruments, her other duties including helping to dress surgeons in their gowns and masks and taking away used instruments for sterilisation together with 'any discarded limbs'. She witnessed many young men with horrific injuries. 'We had very many casualties from air flights and bombing raids. When people had been badly burnt, we used to float them in a bath of water.'

One Red Cross nurse spoke of an additional nightmare encountered in coming home after work late at night, her testimony chillingly matching that of emergency fire services worker Rita Sibbert who told me about an incident that occurred as she was walking to her house in darkness after a shift at her local fire station:

> “I'd spent the evening filling up fire engines with petrol during an air raid. They had to be kept fuelled-up even with the bombs raining down. It was highly dangerous work and I was exhausted. I was walking home after the all-clear when a man attacked me from behind. He caught me by the throat and attempted to get me down. I was angry and I took off my tin helmet and smacked him with it. 'What are you doing?' I shouted. 'You should be ashamed of yourself. Why aren't you out working like the rest of us?' I would have tackled him. I was ready but he ran off. Some of my language wasn't very ladylike.”

Assaults like this led to robberies, rape and even murders although such crimes were rarely publicised in fear of shattering the myth of community harmony.

'I do not think one was afraid for oneself' recalled the Red Cross nurse, 'better to die as the result of action of a brave foe than at the hands of a petty thief. I would have accepted, almost welcomed a bomb or shrapnel that so battered and dented my tin hat – I was so tired, so sickened by the sights of sadness, so weary of the noise, in particular the guns, the cold, the disbelief of ever being warm again, the perpetual darkness, the sadness of hospitals in dim daylight, of men gurgling through ghastly glass tubes (I never minded the spittoons of the cheerful TB men), of the cheers when brave men (human Germans) hurtled to death in a shot-down aircraft – that I longed for peace. But I wanted it to be a clean death – how egotistical – a grain of sand wanting special treatment.'

The large numbers of casualties often swamped hospitals and although staff did their best, some of the less desperate patients had to fend for themselves, Peggy J. Lowthrop from Coniston near Hull recounting her experience in the Hull Royal Infirmary recovering from a fairly minor eye operation:

“Nurses did their best but there were so few of them. I needed my eye bathing frequently but no one was available, so after three days, I pleaded to be allowed home. After a further long wait for the doctor's permission, this was granted but they forgot to 'phone my mother to bring my clothes. I was devastated when she arrived at waiting time, so off she went to collect them. When she returned, she had forgotten some of my important underwear but I was not going to be put off again. I looked for a nurse, but unable to find anyone, I discharged myself and travelled home on the bus in my pyjamas, covered by an overcoat and a large patch over one eye.”

Some patients had pleasanter experiences. The intervention of the war curtailed the promising career of talented golfer Max Faulkner, a job as a physical training instructor with the RAF and a spell in hospital as a consequence of a perforated eardrum, delaying his ambitions for stardom. 'Every morning,' he recalled with nostalgia, 'the nurses brought pretty flowers into the ward and every night they took them out again. It was so grey without those flowers and I thought "if ever I get out of this bloody war, I'm going to wear some colours."' In 1951 a triumphant and flamboyant Max won the Open at Royal Portrush, bedazzling the spectators in an outfit consisting of handmade shoes, a horizontal striped shirt and canary coloured trousers.

The traumas experienced by nurses, who routinely met agonising death on a daily basis, were enormous but the awful sights and sounds had their compensations, student nurse D. K. Warham who worked at Leeds General Infirmary witnessing a veritable miracle in 1942. A young man with blood poisoning was near death, the standard sulphuromide drug treatment of the time doing little to counter the bacterial infection. Enter a team of desperate doctors holding an experimental flask of yellow liquid. This was drip fed into the infected limb '... and there were dramatic signs of improvement' the inflammation subsiding and the temperature dropping. 'It seemed like a miracle. I suppose it was! Because of the legacy, penicillin became used generally very quickly and saved many lives.'

Name: Elsie Trumper
Date of Birth: 27 September 1921
Wartime location: Halifax

“If I'd have thought too much about what I was doing, I'd have wept all the time. But we were too busy. Some of the sights were horrendous but you just got on with it and tried to smile even though you were cut up inside. I wanted to get away at the end of my stint but sometimes I'd linger. Lots of the patients just wanted to talk and to hold your hand – a smile, a laugh, anything really to stop them thinking about the awful state they were in. I remember one young man asking me if he was going to get better. 'Of course you are!' I said cheerily, leaving with a farewell wave of my hand. When I got there next morning, there was someone else in the bed. It was like that all the time. ”

... BANK TELLERS

Rock solid pillars of society, wartime banks were caparisoned like ocean liners, mahogany doors, wainscoting and polished counters, gleaming brass and marble reflecting the sobriety of a profession that, like manager Captain Mainwaring in the BBC series *Dad's Army*, were the epitome of organisation and rectitude. Staff losses to the armed forces led to the recruitment of many women as clerks and tellers, work carrying on as normal despite the constant threat of air raids in the more centrally located branches in city centres. Some of the more vulnerable banks had their own shelters built into basements. Some banks were hit and damaged in overnight raids, stiff upper lips, mops and brooms and yards of boarding ensuring that they were open for business the next day... at ten o'clock sharp!

Banks like *Martins* and the *Yorkshire Penny Bank* whose headquarters was in Leeds offered all the traditional financial services. They were also responsible for the marketing and distribution of National Savings Certificates.

Name: Joyce Eaglestone
Born: 1920
Wartime location: Bradford

“Suddenly ... I was given a three day holiday ... and much good that seemed to me, between boyfriends, in Bradford that oasis of boredom. 'I think I'll go to Morecambe.' I told my parents. I'd heard the RAF had taken over the town and I was in need of a good time. 'You'll not go alone. I'll come with you,' said Mother, and go she did.

We went that Saturday afternoon by train. We found rooms on Sandylands at a bed and breakfast house owned by a Mrs Perkins, a distant cousin of Mother. After our evening meal, I told her I was going to a dance at the Winter Gardens. 'No, go the Pier,' she said. We walked to the Battery still arguing the merits of Pier against Winter Gardens when I saw a bus just about to start. 'See you,' I called and ran for it. I knew she hadn't a hope of catching me.

I'd never been to a dance alone before and my heart gave a flip as I paid my entrance fee – nine old pence for girls and sixpence for men in uniform. This covered the entrance to the theatre where Henry Hall's Guest Night was the star attraction. Almost immediately, a handsome RAF sergeant who was a fantastic dancer claimed me. Rather impeded by my gas mask cum handbag, we quickstepped round the hall until another RAF man cut in. He looked very young, had a cruel haircut, a very new uniform, hobnailed boots and he couldn't dance. 'I was just on my way to the show when I saw you,' he said. 'I'm feeling a bit rough. I've been inoculated in one arm and vaccinated in the other. Shall we go and sit in the balcony?' I was glad to go. I didn't trust those boots for I was wearing fragile sandals. He told me his name, Norman, not a favourite of mine. He held my hand and talked a lot.

We found we had much in common. He had a white mongrel called Tony. I had a black mongrel called Teddy. He walked me back to Mrs Perkins house and we planned to meet the next afternoon. I watched him walk away. Tomorrow, I would see him again. I never doubted that.

Sunday was very sunny and we had a short walk along the promenade but Norman was obviously feeling very ill and was deathly pale. When we reached Sandylands, we sat down on the grass overlooking the sea. 'Don't you think you ought to go sick?' I asked anxiously. He smiled. 'You don't go sick unless you're actually dying. Trouble is, I was never vaccinated as a child so I've had a reaction.

There was another stupendous sunset over Morecambe Bay, such a peaceful world, or so it seemed. Then it was twilight, the summer solstice and barely dark and we had to part. 'I'll not be able to see you till evening tomorrow,' he said. 'There'll be squads of us stamping up and down the promenade with our replica guns. I reckon the real ones were all left behind in France.'

It was the first time I'd really thought of war, of the mayhem just across the Channel. But war seemed very close next day as for what seemed miles along the promenade were men in their blue uniforms. That evening we went straight to our place on the grass. I looked down on this stranger who was now so much part of my life. After the racket of the day it seemed very quiet, the promenade almost deserted except for a family of four, father, mother, and what must have been twin boys who were so fat they could scarcely waddle. 'Just look at those two boys,' I said. 'I'd hate to have fat children like that.' Norman lifted his head and looked. He smiled at me. 'No fear of us having fat children, we're both very slim.' Strange really. I'd come to Morecambe to have a good time and all I'd done was fall in love.

Tuesday was our last evening; we were going home early next day. We exchanged names and addresses and it was then I saw his name written down, Norman Eaglestone, Greenvale, Woodside, Ferndown, Dorset. That was magic compared with Joyce Hanson, Toller Lane, Bradford.

We were married in April 1942 on embarkation leave, but he didn't go abroad until November and that was one bleak Christmas. It was November 1945 before we met again.

I often wonder what my life would have been like if I'd missed that bus. That nine pence I spent that June evening turned out to be a prime investment. ”

(This entry is a condensed version of an article entitled *A Prime Investment* published in issue No. 94 of *Down Your Way* magazine. It is included with the kind permission of its author who enjoyed a long and fruitful Diamond Wedding-attaining marriage with Norman who died in 2002. The couple had three children . . . all slim.)

… AIR TRAINING CORPS TRAINEES

The Air Training Corps scheme was a national initiative offering pre-entry training for boys who wished to join the RAF or the Fleet Air Arm. Boys were directly inducted from high schools and were taught basic aeronautical skills such as flying dynamics and navigation, the more able students going on to actual flying training. By May 1941, 100 eager boys had already enrolled in Air Training Corp N739 Squadron in Scarborough.

Name: Brian Hunter
Born: 1925
Wartime location: Sutton Road, Hull

❝We were having an RAF training lecture one evening when the air raid warning sounded. We carried on with the lecture as nothing seemed to be happening but suddenly guns started firing and we heard bombers. We started to go down the stairs to the shelter. Suddenly, we heard a bomb whistling which meant it was pretty close. We all froze and the whistling got louder. We thought we would be killed. I remember thinking that I'd never get to be a pilot after all. Suddenly, there was a terrific thump and the building shook. We all looked at each other and someone yelled: 'We're still alive!' The bomb had landed about eight to ten feet away from us but hadn't gone off or we'd have all been killed.

Shortly after this everything was quiet even though the all clear hadn't sounded. So we decided to get on our bikes and pedal like mad for home.

I was nearly home when all hell broke loose again – guns, bombs – the lot. I kept my head down and pedalled like mad. I suddenly heard a zip and felt a pain in my forehead. It was a piece of shrapnel; it had cut through my forehead, which was bleeding, and I fell off my bike. If it had been an inch or two further back or I had pedalled one bit further forward, it would have gone through my skull and killed me.

I guess it was my lucky night. I've still got that piece of shrapnel – about three to four inches of jagged metal.❞

... FARMERS' WIVES

Farming was a reserved occupation, the life of the nation depending on home-grown cereals, vegetables, fruit, livestock and poultry at a time when sea import tonnages were dwindling as a consequence of the reduction in the merchant fleet, and the depredations of German surface raiders and U Boats. Nine million acres of land were under cultivation in 1939, a reduction of two million acres in just twenty years. Suddenly, encouraged by a government bounty of £2 for every additional acre put the plough, every available field corner was brought into production. Priority was given to the availability of fertilisers and fuel for tractors and other equipment, British Summer Time was extended to provide more daylight for harvesting and extra labour was mobilised to augment the dwindling numbers of seasonal workers who were conscripted for the armed forces. Thousands of women joined the Land Army, schoolchildren were recruited during the summer months to help bring in the crops and POW labour was extensively used throughout the country, farmers paying a fee to the authorities for the privilege.

Such was the dedication and hard work of farmers, their wives and helpers that by the end of the war, just one third of the nation's food was imported, down from a pre-conflict total of two thirds.

Farmers and their wives worked long hours often seven days a week with few breaks, wives having to provide extra meals to cater for increasing numbers of seasonal workers.

Name: Irene Megginson
Born: 1919
Wartime location: Manor House Farm, Fraisthorpe and South Kingsfield Farm, Boynton

After entertaining an ambition of attending drama school and training as a groom at stables on a Devon Farm, twenty-year-old Irene Oxtoby returned to Yorkshire at the outbreak of war to seek work on the farm of her good friend Jack Megginson. Irene takes up the story:

“I immediately thought of the Megginson's and went by bus to see them (still no telephone in the village) and asked if they could do with a land girl. Nellie said ‘yes’. I could go but they wouldn't pay; it would have to be ‘meat for work.’ Jack was delighted to have me join the workforce and he kept saying in the following months: ‘You should have some remuneration.’

It was almost inevitable too that Jack and I should fall in love and our winter evenings were cosy by the dining room fire where we were often alone. We had an old wireless set and I did patchwork cushions or wrote letters by lamplight. Those wireless programmes meant such a lot to us – apart from the war news. The Tommy Handley – *Much Binding* – and the Western Brothers gave such pleasure. For supper we toasted a teacake and drank mugs of cocoa.

I worked hard on the farm and I even ploughed for the odd half-day. I 'plugged muck', cleaned out hen huts and was generally kept busy feeding the pigs with potatoes. They ate boiled spuds that had been dyed purple for stock identification.

In the bedrooms were marble-topped washstands with large bowls and jugs for washing purposes. In summer, there was plenty of sea bathing which helped keep one clean. There were chamber pots under all the beds to be emptied in slop pails each morning and carried out to empty in the fold yard. Down the garden path were two little 'houses' one with a single hole seat and one with accommodation for two people! These were the bucket variety which also had to be emptied in the yard but the farm men could only use the straw-filled yard or hedges if down the fields We managed in the house with a small amount of milk, often watered down for cooking purposes.

The war was having more impact on us personally, with the threat of invasion as we were only a mile from the coast which had sand dunes rather than cliffs. Concrete posts were erected in the fields between the village and the sea to deter gliders landing. Concrete blocks and barbed wire appeared on the beach and there was a restriction from people visiting within a five mile stretch of the countryside.

We heard on the wireless, that in the case of invasion, women and children would be moved inland, a fact which urged us to marry sooner so we could stay together as a married couple. It really was a very alarming stage of the war for us.

On my twenty-first birthday on 9 March 1940, Jack and I announced our engagement. In spite of many difficulties, we made plans to be married in Barmston church on 25 July 1940. Neither of us wanted any fuss! We would have a small cake, sandwiches with port wine afterwards at Manor House.

I spent a day in Hull to buy some trousseau clothes, mother insisting I have a silk nightie as my pyjamas would not be suitable for a bride. In the weeks before the wedding, I transformed the plain bedroom I'd used since working at Manor Farm. The furniture and carpet couldn't be changed but with matching bedspread and eiderdown and newly made green curtains, I felt the room was more 'me'.

I thought no one outside the village would get to the church but my mother got a permit to enter our restricted zone with a car load. It was all very simple with few spectators but no photographer only the odd box-Brownie snap. On the way to the railway station for our honeymoon in the Lake District, Jack stopped off at the bank to sign a new will, making sure his new wife would inherit! I suppose wartime conditions made one apprehensive and he wasn't taking risks.

When we returned home, the air raids became more regular, at least over Hull and we all slept downstairs. One frightening afternoon, the Battle of Britain took place overhead and ended up with the wreckage of a German fighter plane strewn over fields and bodies in pieces. We huddled in the dark passage and felt sure the Germans had invaded.

We got the tenancy of the South Kingfield Farm on the Boynton Estate from April 1942. No one would live in such a house with one half day cleaning out the filth with complete lack of amenities. Drinking water had to be brought from Manor House as the kind that gushed from the back-kitchen pump was brownish. Over many weeks we got the house in order. We got rid of black beetles with lots of Keating's but some survived until DDT.

We had two men living in and there were men from neighbouring farms to help with threshing and four land girls. The dinner I usually provided was hot meat and tatie pie with rice pudding to follow. As well as the usual meals, they all needed 'lowance' twice daily as in hay time, harvest and muck-leading. So lots of plate pies on the dairy shelf. One harvest in 1943 was memorable for the help we had from the Army. My baking days were even more frantic with twenty-two soldiers extra for 'lowance'. ”

(These extracts, with the kind permission of author Irene Megginson, are taken from her privately published book *A Life on the Wolds – The Story of Jack Megginson*.)

... BAKERS AND CONFECTIONERS

Bread is the staff of life, its continued availability during the war years being essential to feeding the nation and keeping up morale. Bread was never rationed during the conflict although long queues formed outside bakeries from early morning. Ironically, bread was rationed for a brief period after the war in 1946. In 1941 calcium was compulsorily added to flour to counter the onset of rickets, which had been detected as a common aliment afflicting women joining the Land Army. As an economy measure, the National Loaf was introduced in 1942 making use of whole grains and husks in a recipe devised by scientists and the Federation of Bakers who organised production and distribution. The slicing and wrapping of loaves was prohibited at the same. The National Loaf was not universally popular. It was generally regarded as dry and coarse and unappetising, its dirty beige colour proving a turn off for many. The nation was slow to recognise the nutritional value of brown wholemeal bread despite the findings of scientists who championed consumption for health reasons. Its compulsory introduction brought improvements in wellbeing particularly amongst children, an advertising campaign by the Ministry of Food including the following jingle:

Pat-a-loaf, pat-a-loaf
Baker's man,
Bake me some wheatmeal
As fast as you can:
It builds up my health
And it tastes so good,
I find that I like
Eating just what I should.

The National Loaf was finally abandoned in 1956.

Name: Charlie Hitchen
Born: 3 August 1915
Wartime location: Thurlstone, near Penistone

"I left Thurlstone Church of England School at fourteen years of age and started work in May 1930 at a small cottage bakery run by two sisters. They gave me two baskets, one filled with bread and plain and currant teacakes and the other with confectionery. They set me off on foot on a round of local houses, giving me a money bag filled with change. Eventually, they bought me a three-wheeled little handcart. Trays of sweet cakes and pastries were kept inside. The bread and teacakes were carried in cardboard boxes on top. The cart enabled me to extend my rounds. I usually carried between eight and ten dozen loaves but the potholes were even worse in the old days and if I hit one, then the door would fly open and the trays would shoot out. Thankfully, on a dry day, I would pick the goods up and dust them down. Some days I did Thurlstone and parts of Millhouse. On other days I went to Penistone (we did school dinners for the poor children of the town), Cubley, Castle Green and as far away as Oxspring. That was a seven mile round trip and I pushed my cart there and back all the way. On that run, a customer would know my time and he'd whisk me up an egg in milk. Other kind customers would give me cups of tea as I munched away on currant teacakes – I was allowed the odd one. After work, I'd get back and father would boil me an egg with toast and cheese for my tea. Then, twice a week, I'd run all the way to Penistone Bridge End to catch the six o'clock bus to Huddersfield College where I did practical baking one night and cookery science the next.

In 1934, the sisters decided to give up, leaving me with the choice of finding a place to start my own business. I was good at icing cakes – although the sisters were a little resentful – and at baking. I was taught to bake from an early age and I had to do a lot at home to help look after grandma. Dad encouraged me as well. I had to learn after school using a side oven. When the sisters' retired I found an empty doctor's surgery in Thurlstone and dad asked the doctor if we could rent the place. He agreed. A local flourmill owner lent us the money to pay builders to move the oven and everything else, although it was all baking by hand in those days.

So, I got going and bought an electric mixer. Then a little Morris van. It was not really big enough so I paid £100 for a Ford. I wished many times over I hadn't bought it for if it got damp it wouldn't start up at all. I started making my own little meat pies. I delivered them hot to people who were working overtime at the nearby umbrella factory.

Then a shop became vacant on Penistone High Street. I took it and tried one or two assistants but with the war now on, rationing took its toll and the shop closed and with shortages of fuel, the van was put into a garage. I continued baking of course. We were allowed a certain amount of raw materials but it was very basic. We only had margarine and very little lard just some sort of substitute. And no icing sugar. People queued down the street waiting for the bread to be ready. Around that time, I met my wife to be Violet at a village hall dance. I found out later that Violet, being the eldest had to learn to bake just like me.

I received my call up papers around April 1941. I joined the Catering Corp and was posted all the way to the Orkney Islands. Violet and I had been courting two or three years by this time – she often helped me at the weekends cleaning and swilling out – and she went to work in the bake house while I was away. I was away on and off from 1941 to 1946 living the life of Reilly. I was the cook for two officers and a batman. When I went to Orkney I was just under ten stones. When I came home, I was touching the thirteen stone mark. I didn't know what war was.

When I demobbed, I had to adjust. Violet had a few words to say to me about settling down and getting stuck in. You know what lovers do after words. So, eventually we bought a rambling place called Junction House on the moors at Hade Edge above Holmfirth and converted it to a bakery and teashop and our home after we got married. And that winter of 46/47 was the worst of last century. We had to sledge the bread to Dunford Station, Townhead and Carlecotes. I can honestly say I never let a customer down come hail, blow or snow. In one spell, we worked seven days a week for seven years without a break. Sometimes, Ashley Jackson – he's famous now for his moorland scenes – would come and sit in our café corner on a grey day. We carried on until 1969, new fangled food and health regulations forcing us out of business.

During the last five years, I met two lady sisters who were pleased to see me again after nearly seventy years. They remembered me going through Springvale on my way to Oxspring with my little handcart. They even recall the sweet cakes and teacakes their mother bought from me. They worked in the factory at Millhouse. It didn't have a canteen so if they had to work over, someone would telephone and order hot meat pies. I'd deliver them in the van and they'd eat them at their benches. To be remembered and respected after all this time means a lot to me.

I still like good bread. I do my own baking – brown teacakes, and currant teacakes – two dozen at a time. I'm very fortunate. I say thanks morning and night for my health and strength.”

The following report appeared in a local newspaper in March 1947:

“BAKER GETS THROUGH: During the recent blizzard, Mr Charles Hitchin, baker of Thurlstone, set out to supply bread to the people of Dunford but was only able to reach Carlecotes by road before he was compelled to turn back. Mr Hitchen returned to Penistone station and set off by passenger train to Dunford with his supplies but on his arrival at Dunford, the blizzard had increased to such an intensity that rail traffic was suspended and Mr Hitchen was compelled to spend the night in a signal box at Dunford station. This is the second occasion during the recent severe weather that Mr Hitchen has made the journey to Dunford with much needed supplies.”

. . . STOKERS

On the footplates of steam engines, in the bowels of tramp steamers and in the boiler rooms of a myriad wartime factories and hospitals, apprentices soon learnt to appreciate the difference between a spade and a shovel, long repetitive hours of rhythmic stoking and raking in blisteringly hot, gas and dust-ladened conditions, causing burns and lesions and leading to joint and respiratory conditions exacerbated, long term, by the insinuating problems of asbestos. Stokers, the unseen and unheralded fire-ants of the war period, really kept the home fires burning.

Name: Robert Issac Rawson
Born: 26 March 1904
Wartime location: Horseman Avenue, Cemetery Road, York
(Memories recalled by his daughter Barbara Pettitt)

“My father worked as a stoker and Acting Clerk of Works at the Imphal Barracks and Military Hospital in Fulford Road, York and Hospital Fields for forty-five years. He obtained the Imperial Service Medal from the Queen for loyal services to the Crown. He used to look after eleven boilers and maintain all the buildings within the boundaries of the cook houses and make sure the water was hot at all times for the army and civilian workforce. He worked terribly hard on shifts seven days a week and he was always on call in case of air raids. He had to move a ton of coke every day and barrow it into the boiler house underneath the cookhouse or hospital buildings. He used to smoke to hide the smell of the coke gases as it made him cough a lot. He was never off sick in all his forty-five years. Dad used to bring home cinders from work to eke out our coal ration. He gave some to old folks in a bucket with chopped sticks to make a fire.

We had two Jewish ladies next door who used to swap fat, bacon and sweet coupons in return for tea, soap, margarine and washing powder. They were called Hannah and Sarah Cohen. In 1943, they were scared that Hitler was going to come from Germany into the UK. One morning, my dad noticed the curtains were still closed. He knocked on the door – no answer. He called at the police box up the road. They came and found both sisters dead. Hannah had her head on a cushion in the gas oven. Sarah lay on the floor near the fireside with the gas poker to her mouth unlit. They were lovely folks – seamstresses by trade.

My father won the Imperial Services Medal. I was so proud of him. After forty-five years of devoted work tending eleven boilers he died of cancer from inhaling coke fumes and contact with asbestos.

I always surprise them when I say to folk,
That at bath-time, in wartime, I had a good soak,
And splashed all alone in a wonderful tub,
With plenty of time to wallow and scrub.
Happy bath-time memories are the ones for me.

Even though Churchill himself had decreed,
'Five inches of water is all that you need',
There was queuing and rationing, shortage of grub,
But whatever happened, I had a good scrub.
Happy bath-time memories are the ones for me.

My dear old Dad helped Hitler's defeat,
By serving the barracks maintaining the heat.
So while all my school friends took baths in a crowd,
We had a bathroom of which we were proud.
Happy bath-time memories are the ones for me.

We might have been hungry; we might have been poor,
But just like the Navy, we 'splashed' through the War.
Soaking in Lux Flakes and Pears 'Golden Glory',
Barbara was happy for you to hear her story,
Happy bath-time memories are the ones for me. ”

(Barbara Pettitt)

... FACTORY WORKERS

Labour shortages became so acute as ever more manpower was conscripted to the military, that in May 1941 it became compulsory for all women aged between nineteen and forty to register at employment exchanges. This enabled the Ministry of Labour to direct women into 'essential work'. Many employers were sceptical about the ability of females to take on demanding physical work but under the duress of the Essential Work Order, they had no option but to recruit women. A typical scene involved scores of women bent over their production lines filling munitions, other work involving turning, drilling, filing, screwing, soldering, assembling, sorting and packing as they listened to *Music While You Work* over the loudspeakers. Popular songs of the period were *Yours*, *I'll Be Seeing You* and *We'll Meet Again*. Some women trained for more exacting work, a party of Yorkshire ladies from Penistone and Huddersfield becoming highly skilled welders, working on the production of bailey bridges in Huddersfield. Some fortunate workers were allocated to so-called 'glamour jobs', hundreds of women building bombers at the AVRO factory near Leeds (more than 5,000 aircraft of differing types were made at the factory between 1940 and 1946) and hundreds more assembling the X craft midget submarines at the Broadbent plant in Huddersfield where there was a mighty hurrah on the factory floor on 22 September 1943 after a Tannoy announcement that one of the firm's boats had helped sink the German warship *Tirpitz*. In the centre of Leeds, the specialist optical instrument maker Kershaw's produced prisms for analysing high altitude reconnaissance photographs taken by the RAF and they also produced periscopes for battle tanks. Some jobs were more dangerous than others. One Sheffield lady spoke of the dangers of operating dangerous machinery producing shell casings, on one occasion, red-hot slivers of metal flying out from the lathe, perforating her cheek and knocking her teeth out in a torrent of blood. After a few stitches, she was back at her lathe the next morning. Other similarly vulnerable ladies who were accidentally asphyxiated by mustard gas at the ICI factory in Huddersfield were evacuated to the nearby moors above the Colne Valley to recuperate.

Without women, Britain's factories would have quickly ground to a halt and the push against Nazism would have been stunted. Although female workers initially had many detractors, Labour leader Clement Atlee spoke for the nation in 1942, declaring: 'The work that women are performing in munitions factories has to be seen to be believed.' Tremendously hard working, skilful and totally committed to the cause, women often laboured under primitive and dangerous conditions but they did so with a quip and a smile, singing:

I'm only a wartime girl
The machine shop makes me deaf,
I've no prospects after the war
And my young man is in the RAF
K for Kitty calling, P for Prue ... bomb doors open ...
Over to you ...

Name: Ethel Elizabeth Markham
Born: 4 July 1911
Wartime location: Bertha Street, Richmond Hill, Leeds
(Memories recalled by the author)

"My mother lived in a community of back-to-back houses on what was known as The Bank in East Leeds in an area dominated by the imposing presence of Mount St Mary's Catholic Church. My sister Maureen was a young girl at the outbreak of war, both my parents working in the clothing trade, my father Leonard as a cloth cutter and my mother as a seamstress at Burton's tailors at the sprawling Hudson Road works. Like his brothers, my father volunteered for the navy and was enlisted on 19 May 1941. Initially he was posted to the Orkney Islands on harbour defence duties but eventually he went to sea as an able seaman aboard a modern aircraft carrier, HMS *Implacable* seeing service with the British Pacific Fleet and action against Japanese home islands between July and August 1945. Like hundreds of thousands of wives across the nation, my mother stiffened her upper lip and got on with things, working long hours in the factory making uniforms and other clothing for the war effort and bringing up my sister. The Bertha's were home to predominately Catholic families and the large contingent of Irish priests worked hard to maintain the faith and morale, counselling those ladies in the parish who received the dreaded telegrams. The only contact British forces had with their families was by censored letter, many homesick serviceman writing home every week. The letter reproduced here from my father is typical of the many millions sent during the war years:

151 Coast Battery
Stromness
Orkneys
My own Ethel. Well my darling there were no pictures last night so I went to bed early as I was on duty at twelve. There is nowhere to go here so we might as well turn in early. I'm getting quite a champ at dominoes these days. We also have a dartboard, so you can see this is how we spend our time.

How do you manage for getting the coal these days when you are always at work and other things for your everyday needs?

I see that Maureen is coming on a great deal with her lessons at school. I was very pleased to hear it. Tell her that dad is always thinking about her. I see that she is still enjoying the sweets and going to the pictures and according to what you say she is in the best of health.

I can assure you that when this lot is all over and Mr Hitler is just a memory, we will be the happiest family in the world.

I will leave you with the same old words. Keep your chin up because I love you. Good night. God Bless. Keep you safe.

Len"

Name: Ethel Thompson
Born: 1920
Wartime location: Huntington

"I started work at Rowntree's* at the age of fourteen in 1934 and was still there making fancy boxes for the chocs when war broke out. I went to live with my sister in the old village of Huntington to keep her company. I remember some local ladies coming with a list wanting places for evacuees and yes; my sister said we'd take two little ones. So came a little girl of about seven and her little brother of five from Middlesbrough. The little lad had a dummy still and his sister used to secretly give it to him every night. We sometimes entertained the local soldiers from nearby Strensall camp and although we hadn't much to offer, I remember making coconut cakes with liquid paraffin for fat from the chemist. It tasted fine!

We had two village pubs. I was treated to a few Guinness's for strength. One elderly chap – on request – sang *When the Sergeant Major's on Parade* almost every Sunday in *The Blacksmith's*. We were always a bit short on glasses and would carry them between the two pubs.

I don't remember much Black Market but once I was offered two white vests without clothing coupons and when I looked in the mirror, their whiteness revealed my orange tan! I had become jaundiced. Almost immediately, I got bad shingles but the medical care I received was the best.

People were chummy. I remember once when my parents hurriedly got into their shelter, Billy the postman next door shouted: 'Want a cup of tea Winnie?' over the hedge."

* Rowntree's turned over some of their storage areas for the war effort, the 'Smarties Block' converting for optical instrument assembly and fuse filling.

Name: Peggy J. Lowthrop
Born: 1920
Wartime location: Coniston, Hull

"I spent almost forty-five years working at Rosedown's in Hull. Travelling to and from work in Hull needed a sense of humour and a good level of fitness. The old double-deckers had a running board on them and many times coming home at teatime so many people were standing on these that the running boards only just cleared the road. And, of course, inside you could hardly move. The drivers knew us well and were eager to get us home, so they promised that if we waited a few yards away from the bus stop they would slow down just sufficiently for us to jump on, leaving people they didn't know at the official stop. Coming home on a foggy night was also an experience. With compulsory dimming of the bus lights the drivers had a tough job but they were very determined – particularly when they lived in Hornsea. I was one of several passengers who took it in turns to walk in front of the bus for up to a mile to guide the driver.

I was also a member of the firm's first aid team and I was involved in another first aid team for Coniston village. One Sunday morning a mock invasion was staged. My sister and I were told to collect a casualty from a field behind the village. We got him on a stretcher but then had to negotiate a stile to get back to the village hall. He was of somewhat large proportions and it was going to be difficult. Realising this, he piped up, 'I'm not going to let two young lassies like you lift me over that. I'll get off and you can put me back on t'other side.' We duly did so and on reaching the hall were very surprised to see the 'Germans' and our men supping cups of tea together! It transpired that about a mile from the village, the 'Germans' had commandeered the milk van and knowing how essential it was for the villagers to get their daily pinta, our lads had waved it through without another glance.

I was in charge of the Brownie Pack (Brown Owl) during the war. Because we couldn't have the children out at night, all our uniformed groups met on a Saturday. It was so essential to keep the children's lives as normal as possible and we had great fun. One afternoon, I realised that several of them had disappeared. I found them outside staging a bridal procession and presenting the 'bride' with a wedding present – a rusty birdcage they'd found in a rubbish bin. All this had arisen because there was a wedding in church and they had seen the real bride arriving!"

Names: Dennis Bedford and Doris Bedford
Born: 1921 and 1923
Wartime location: Clayton West and Kexborough, Barnsley
(Memories recalled by their son Barry Bedford)

"In the early part of the war, my dad worked in the offices of the Naylor Pipeworks in Denby Dale. He often told me about his rather hot courting days when, after work, he'd set off on foot from his house in Clayton West to meet my mother in Kexborough sometimes during an air raid. He must have been smitten. To dodge the shrapnel from the bombs and the anti aircraft shells, he'd skip over a wall and lay low in a wood for fifteen minutes. After joining the RAF, dad went off to Africa and mum went to work for Rolls Royce in Barnoldswick*.

Rolls Royce developed one of the world's first jet engines although mum didn't know what she was working on at the time. She worked there during the week and stayed in the firm's hostel. Her most vivid memories were of the journeys home at the weekends. On Friday nights, they travelled in a double-decker bus from the factory to Bradford and then on to Barnsley and district dropping off girls and singing popular songs all the way. On occasions they would stay over and visit Manchester, Blackburn and Preston to enjoy the dance bands touring at the time.

Dad and several of his pals volunteered for the RAF in 1942 and dad somehow found himself doing training in Blackpool. He had a most imposing Drill Sergeant – Brian London, the famous boxer. With his new-found friend John Beanland, dad had to guard the Blackpool Football Stadium. Just the two of them. One was on the outside and the other on the inside. With a serious look on his face, dad always insisted that no German could ever have got in. 'If they'd somehow managed to get past me, they would then have had to face John ... and they'd never have got past him.' Dad and John eventually went abroad and spent some time in Rhodesia. They remained lifelong friends and often talked about how rough the war was out there as they only had a choice of three types of beer. After leaving the UK, the nearest action they saw was when their convoy was attacked by a U-boat. The U-boat was sunk. They did their bit and had no choice of where they were sent, so I suppose like everyone else they made the best of what they had. They were young men full of mischief. Neither dad nor John was musical but they joined a band as trumpeters (they pretended to blow) to get out of Sunday duties.

The one message that came from mum and dad loud and clear was that the war years bred such a local spirit of goodwill. Everybody helped everybody else."

* Bankfield Mill in Barnoldswick, Lancashire was originally a cotton mill. It was bought by Rover in 1941 and sold to Rolls Royce in April 1943, brilliant Chief Engineer Dr Stanley Hooker pioneering improvements in the Merlin engine for Spitfires and Hurricanes and improving efficiency by 30 per cent. By 1944 over 2,000 personnel – many of these were from across the county boundary in Yorkshire – were working at the top-secret plant, 1,500 of the best operatives, on twelve hour round-the-clock shifts, manufacturing turbine blades for the revolutionary B23 – the Welland – the power unit for the Gloster Meteor jet aircraft. This was the only allied jet to see operational service during World War Two.

TELEGRAM

10th August 1944

To the staff and workers at Messrs Rolls Royce, Barnoldswick. I can now tell you – please do not repeat it outside the factory – that your engines are in operation against the enemy.

My heartfelt congratulations to everyone whose work has contributed to this fine result. This is only the beginning and we want all the spares and additional engines that you can raise for us as soon as possible. I know I can rely on you to do your part.

Sir Stafford Cripps
Ministry of Aircraft Production

... BUS CONDUCTRESSES

In the days before drivers performed the dual roles of driving and collecting fares, conductresses were an indispensable part of the transport services. They worked on buses, trams and trolley buses, escorting passengers to their seats, collecting money in big leather satchels and issuing tickets from neck-draped machines that weighed pounds. Ancillary duties including controlling passenger numbers to ensure that the vehicle was not over loaded and ringing bells, signalling to the bus driver to stop and go. If the testimony of Don Bullock (see entry under the heading 'Days in the Lives of . . . Schoolboys and Schoolgirls') is to be believed, conductresses had another function.

❝In 1940, the trolley buses in Mexborough had a bumper on each corner at the rear. We would lay in wait of the tracky setting off, then run up behind, hang onto the bumper, feet off the ground as it picked up speed, and ride to the next stop. I'm sure the conductresses informed the driver if they saw us hanging on, because they used driving tactics to make us fall off.❞

Name: Connie Hold
Born: Not known.
Wartime location: Royston, Barnsley

❝Our main difficulty was getting to and from the depot. Luckily, I had a bicycle. Even then, I had to get up at 3.30 am to be at work for 5.30 am and it was not so easy for girls who had to walk along the lonely roads at that time in a morning. Also, if you were on 'spare' duty, you had to be there by 4.30 am.

We used to take passengers to local pits, to the steelworks at Stocksbridge, the mills at Scissett and the arsenal at Thorpe Arch. Six busloads went to the ICI plant in Huddersfield. Some of them were converted to ambulances and they helped in emergencies like the Sheffield Blitz. There was a shortage of cleaners at the depot so we had to clean our own buses.

We were also engaged on troop ferrying duties including taking American soldiers to Langsett. We saw some disgraceful scenes in the way the white American soldiers treated the dark ones and white and dark were never allowed on the same buses.

Seats were arranged all round the bus sides to allow the maximum numbers of passengers. That's why they called them 'cattle trucks'.

We particularly enjoyed visiting the various collieries in the district because the food was so good. They had lovely meals and we got them at colliers' prices so they were better than having to take packed meals.

Only workers were allowed to travel on the buses after 8.00 pm but many people – especially the 'street ladies' tried it on. They were darlings really.”

(This is an edited extract from an article that appeared in a special supplement of the *Barnsley Chronicle*: *Barnsley at War* published on 1 September 1989)

... HOME GUARDS

The concept of raising a local defence force composed of men unsuitable for front line duties pre-dated the war, one motivational radio broadcast by Secretary of State for War, Anthony Eden on 14 May 1940 heralding the creation of the Local Defence Volunteers. Initially dubbed the 'Last Desperate Venture', the 'Luck, Duck and Vanish Brigade', 'The Long Dentured Veterans' and latterly 'Dad's Army', the organisation soon took on Winston Churchill's original name of the Home Guards. Thousands of men who were too old for combat joined the ranks of pimply youths and short sighted, asthmatic, cack-handed military rejects who flooded to the recruiting stations causing initial widespread panic amongst the generals. By the end of May around 300,000 men had joined the Home Guard and by August over a million volunteers were preparing to repel the invaders using primitive and improvised weapons including English Civil War inspired pikes (250,000 were ordered in July 1941, the armourers uniting scaffolding poles with army surplus bayonets), the Woolworth or Thermos Bomb ('just a lump of gelignite in a biscuit tin'), and the fourgasse (a large oil drum filled with a mixture of petrol and tar detonated by a grenade, it's firing pin attached to a long cord). Each man was issued with a haversack containing a 'tin filled with small bits of metal which when shaken vigorously sounded vaguely like a machine gun.' The Germans were highly amused at the panoply of their opponents' arms scoffing during one propaganda broadcast:

> “Under what arms? Broomsticks, or the arms of the local pub with pots of beer and darts in their hands?”

The recruits were far from cowed, however, and they were, for the most part, deadly serious in their attitudes and training, responsibilities including defending bridges, aerodromes and factories, guarding fuel dumps and key installations, keeping watch on vulnerable coastlines and manning roadblocks, their deployment releasing professional and conscripted soldiers for combat.

Platoons of eager volunteers were formed all over Yorkshire. They were initially a rag-bag assemblage dressed in home-made uniforms although the millionaire tailoring magnate Sir Montague Burton provided 1,500 sets of well-cut battledresses for his local unit in Harrogate, tailors producing the smartest outfits using officer grade barathea cloth. Neatly dressed in their own plus fours, the fifty-seven members of the Cobble Hall Golf Club near Leeds, stoutly resolved to defend their greens to the last tee, devising a regular routine to thwart the Nazi paratrooper scourge that had so devastated France and the Low Countries, four man squads playing eighteen holes before setting out on their patrols. Camaraderie throughout the Home Guard was generally excellent one Yorkshire battalion, the 43rd West Riding, even having it's own drinking song, sung to the tune of *Here's a Health to His Majesty*:

Here's a Health unto the Forty-third:
With a fal la-la,
Confusion to the Axis herd,
With a fal . . . la.
With Keates* and Frost* we do not care
If Jerry comes by sea or air;
The Forty-third will comb their hair,
With a fal . . . la.

The Forty-third West Riding Batt.
With a fal . . . la,
Will knock Herr Schicklegruber flat,
With a fal . . . la.
We'll take his paratroopers for a ride,
We'll do our best to tan their hide,
And send them swimming back next tide,
With a fal . . . la.

The Forty-third's a damn fine crush,
With a fal . . . la,
We'll do our job without a fuss,
With a fal . . . la.
And when we've finished with the Boche,
We'll toast ourselves in gin and squash,
And when we're drunk we'll sing this tosh,
With a fal . . . la.

* Battalion Commander and his Second-in-Command.

Thousands of young boys were recruited to assist the Home Guard. They joined the Army Cadet Corps, one medical student, Michael L. Ryder who was studying hard at Leeds University in September 1944, recalling: '. . . what seems incredible now . . . I actually kept a .303 Lee Enfield rifle in my bedroom at home!'

Name: Robert Markham
Born: 28 March 1926
Wartime location: Daisy Hill, Drax

“I left school in 1941 and started work as an apprentice fitter at Olympia Cake and Oil Company in Selby. It was a forty-five hour week and the take home pay was 14s/8d.The distance to work was nine miles which I cycled. I joined the Home Guard on 16 May 1942 – A Company 10th West Riding Selby Battalion. I was now sixteen years old and carrying arms – a .300 Canadian Ross rifle, later a .303 Lee-Enfield. During the war, the Hull & Barnsley Railway was brought back into service. It was the requirement of the Home Guard to defend the swing bridge at Long Drax (Langrick) that carried the railway over the Ouse. Having studied First Aid, my main job was medical in the platoon until it was disbanded on 31 December 1944. I had been deferred from active service until I finished my apprenticeship. I was the treasurer of the local youth club and organised dances in aid of the Forces Fund. The proceeds were shared between all the local service men and women annually. I was also a chorister at St Peter and St Paul's Church, Drax. On Saturday afternoons, I spent time in the workshops at Selby Technical College machining parts for the war effort. The output was taken to the tank factory at Barnbow in Leeds. I was an extremely busy young man. Every night I was out and on Sunday mornings I was on parade but I still didn't qualify for a Defence Medal. ”

Name: Eric Lord
Born: Not known
Wartime location: Hull

“The platoon to which I was detailed was composed of quite an assortment of characters. There was the company director, the labourer, the office worker and a whole host of other occupations were represented. There were, of course, quite a number of First World War veterans and they contrasted sharply with the band of young fellows who had all the arrogance of youth.

We of the youthful segment enjoyed our times on parade and the limited exercises. Perhaps we swaggered a little. I made some good pals and we joked that we would defend battle headquarters, the *Three Tuns Hotel*, to the last pint. There is a confession here that I was an under-age drinker, but in social outings to pubs and dances there was never any bad behaviour from anyone. In that environment and at that time, one very rarely heard someone swear.

The most humorous incident concerning life in the Home Guard was related to me from a member of a platoon whose duties involved defence of the Kirkella (an outlying district of Hull) area. This platoon built a road block near the golf course and any traffic had to negotiate a passage through strategically placed farm carts. After completion of this obstacle, the platoon officer gathered the men around him to discuss their efforts and the efficacy of the structure.

'What do you all think of it?' he queried beaming with all the satisfaction of having helped to promote a major bulwark defying the onslaught of the Nazi hordes. My informant had the temerity to pipe up and pose a question to the officer.

'Excuse me sir, but I don't quite understand. What's to stop any German tanks just ignoring the road block and crossing the golf course?'

'Crossing the golf course! Crossing the golf course!' thundered the officer. 'They wouldn't dare!' ”

Name: Joseph Ormrod
Born: Not known
Wartime location: Darfield, Barnsley

“ One Sunday morning we were attacking Thurnscoe, and Westland Lysander aircraft were dropping bags of flour as bombs. We had been ordered to capture the railway bridge near a pub nicknamed *The Drum*. We had succeeded in capturing it when someone looked at his watch and said: 'Eh-up, it's ten past twelve.' Everyone left the bridge and from then on the war finished at 12.00 noon every Sunday.

One dark moonless night, we were supposed to capture another platoon that was somewhere in the vicinity of Cat Hill, at Broomhill. As we approached where we thought they were we heard a slight hissing sound from the other side of the wall. The sergeant whispered that it was somebody relieving himself, so we leapt over the wall and into the attack – to find ourselves surrounding a road roller with a jet of steam escaping from it.

Weapons and field training were the sergeant's specialities. One day, demonstrating the .303 Lee-Enfield and stressing the importance of checking that the breech was empty before squeezing the trigger, he suited the actions to the words and shot a hole through the ceiling.

He was equally gifted in the field. We were attacking Salt Pie Farm at Mitchell's and were creeping in pitch darkness through the old keeper's field at Darfield. Our sergeant asked: Do you know where you are lads?' and we all answered: 'Yes'. He asked the same question several times and when he got the same answer for the fourth or fifth time, he said: 'Where the bloody well are we then . . . 'cos I'm lost.' ”

Mrs Ormrod was never enamoured at the Home Guard exploits of her three young sons. On the day war ended, she bundled up all the ammunition amassed by the boys and dumped it in the River Dearne.

(This is an edited extract from an article that appeared in a special supplement of the *Barnsley Chronicle*: *Barnsley at War* published on 1 September 1989)

... MEMBERS OF THE WOMEN'S VOLUNTARY SERVICE

The Women's Voluntary Service was set up at the instigation of the Home Office in 1938. The intention was to mobilise women over the age of conscription, those not directed into war work, or mothers who had family commitments, recruits offering a wide range of social services. By August 1939, the WVS had attracted 336,000 volunteers nationwide, this number rising to a million by May 1941.

The WVS ladies wore a dapper green uniform and a brimmed hat, sporting a distinctive red band and a WVS badge, the army of Florence Nightingales offering cheery smiles and mugs of tea when the war weary flagged the most. They greeted men returning from the front and blitz victims with hot drinks, blankets, buns and sandwiches. They distributed emergency clothing, organised transport and car pools, set up nurseries for working mums, helped run centres for orphaned or displaced children, counselled old people during air raids, established Emergency Enquiry Points at the sites of major incidents and did a thousand and one other tasks. Sometimes they were charged with breaking the awful news about fatalities to victims' families. They did all this with sensitivity, patience and good humour without pay or other reward, 241 of their number loosing their lives during the conflict.

The WVS group of ladies in Scarborough was outstandingly successful in providing support services. Typically, in January 1945, they organised a convoy of aid for bombed out residents of Finsbury in London, ten van loads taking welcome gifts and furniture. In December of that year, they were recognised in an official report as the 'Show Centre' of the North Riding.

Name: Hilda Appelby
Born: 1902
Wartime location: Fulford, York
(From an original hand written manuscript provided by Hilda's niece Mrs Jean Mordue)

"At the beginning of the war, I was told by a lady that they were desperate for help in the canteen on York Station so I immediately became a member of the WVS. The canteen was built on platform 8 and it never closed from its opening in 1939 until late 1946. Our night shift was the longest and often the busiest of them all – lots of troop movements took place at night.

A taxi picked a friend and I up at a quarter to midnight and the staff we relieved were taken home in the same taxi. There were usually five on our shift and we served tea and coffee, pork pies, sausage rolls and various sandwiches and the most popular of all Spam and beans. Everything was sold just to cover costs as all labour was voluntary. I can still remember standing at a table chopping up Spam at 3.00 to 4.00 am in the morning. The air was so thick with cigarette smoke one could have cut it with a knife.

We would get a message telling us that a troop train would be arriving at a certain time, with perhaps 500 troops on it. We had to prepare stacks of food, urns of tea and coffee all ready for serving quickly. We had to resort many times to jam jars as we ran out of cups. Our losses were enormous – 500 to 600 per month. I have a lovely memory of collecting cups early one morning when I came across a group of soldiers who were on their way to Malaya. One had a saxophone and they were singing and asked me to join them. I sat down with them on a barrow and I was asked for a special request. I chose *Fascinating You*. It always remained a very nostalgic memory.

The Red Cross trains came too. We had to take trays with huge jugs of tea and coffee on these trains, as they were often full of badly injured stretcher cases. This was a very sad job for us but we had to put on a smile, whatever we were feeling.

Another job I did was welfare clothing. We collected masses of clothing which we gave to people who came with notes from doctors, vicars, district nurses and others in authority. Canada and America sent us tons of clothing, shoes and boots.

One welfare afternoon, a very shabby man came in without his letter of authority or recommendation. He asked if we had any men's clothing as he had the chance of a job starting next day. Unfortunately, we hadn't anything for large men that day. I thought quickly and gave him 6d and the directions to my bus stop also telling him how to get to my house and when to get off the bus. I was on my bicycle and decided that if I left straight away I could get home before him. I managed to get there first and put the kettle on and make him some tea and sandwiches. While he was having these on the doorstep, I rushed round my neighbours and begged what men's clothing I could. I managed to acquire underwear, coat, shirts, trousers, socks, boots an overcoat and even two hankies; also a selection of jumpers. After he had finished his tea, I gave him the bundle of clothes and asked him to go into the garage and put on what he required. I hardly knew him when he came out. About four days later as I came home from town, I passed him with a lot of workmen leaving work in the clothes I had given him.

We had large quantities of dried milk, tinned fruit and tinned meat sent to us by the Commonwealth. We distributed these to needy people old and young. Another similar duty was the distribution of food parcels from New Zealand and Canada.

One time, we were asked to give canning demonstrations. America sent us a canning machine and an enormous supply of cans. The public were invited to bring their own fruit and buy the cans from us. This was very popular with housewives. I too was glad to take advantage of using the machine for myself as tinned fruit was impossible to buy at the time.

We had a clothing exchange scheme which was very popular with mothers of young families. Donated surplus clothing would earn you points, which you could accumulate and trade for other clothing. This worked very well and was really appreciated when clothing was on coupons.

Another job I enjoyed was the escorting of displaced persons. I would travel down to Cambridge by train – collect fifty to sixty men for transit to Sutton-on-Derwent. They were given an outfit of clothes, a ration book, clothing coupons, pocket money an English dictionary or simple phrase book and, what was most important of all – an identity card. It was pathetic to see them taking it out of their pockets looking at it over and over again. After a week or two, we would take them on to various places to take up some work. When they came to England, they were only allowed to be miners, hospital workers or agricultural workers. I have had lawyers, doctors, a professor of music and a ballet dancer on my list of displaced persons but even so, they were all very glad to be in England. One Christmas, I invited two women from the camp to my home for dinner and tea. My husband collected them after they had been to a service at York Minster and took them back to the camp at the end of the day (using his precious petrol which was still available to private motorists but which was stopped in mid 1942). I was very touched when they gave me a small parcel. In it was a tablet of toilet soap and a small piece of washing soap.

I also did a bit of liaison work in connection with the Army. My job was to visit soldiers who were to be discharged after being wounded. Maybe they had lost an arm or a leg and I had to see how they were preparing to settle down in civvy life and find out if we could help in any way. We could refer them to their own WVS in their home towns.

Some of my duties – welfare clothing, clothing exchanges, selling National Savings Stamps, old peoples clubs, hospital trolley services – continued right through the war and after. When I agreed to join the WVS I never realised that it would lead to such a variety of jobs. I enjoyed every minute of my service and wouldn't have missed any one of them. ”

... WOMEN'S LAND ARMY GIRLS

Hundreds of farms across Britain were robbed of agricultural labour to serve the all-demanding needs of the armed services, older workers and farmers and their wives having to work harder and longer to produce vital food for the nation. Overwhelming manpower shortages, however, threatened to reduce yields at a time of overwhelming demand and over 20,000 Land Army Girls were recruited to help feed the nation.

Employment was of four types – dairy farming, general farming, market gardening and forestry, girls being allocated to their duties according to previous occupations and physical abilities. Training lasted one month, recruits receiving tuition and 10s per week before they were allocated to a workplace. Usually, if it could be arranged, this was near home, girls commuting daily by bicycle. Other girls were relocated and billeted in purpose-built hostels or in cottages with the wives of farm labourers.

The girls worked a minimum forty-eight hour week with plenty of overtime, receiving around 32s per week. They were all issued with shirts, dungarees, pullovers, stockings, gumboots and oilskin mackintoshes.

Initially, the girls were dismissed as empty-headed pseudo milkmaids and shepherdesses, the more cruel observers disparagingly coining a mocking Land Army motto 'Backs to the Land'.

Land army girls were directed to Yorkshire's agricultural areas by the hundred, the flat lands of Holderness, the Wolds, the Vale of York and the distant Dales all experiencing the friendly invasion with wry smiles and some scratched heads. Farmers were occasionally hostile to the newcomers but the remarks of one Dales farmer were typically upbeat:

“Aye, I don't know what we should have done without 'em. There are many tons of potatoes as would never have been lifted, and a few cows milked if I hadn't had 'em to help. In my view, women have a real knack with animals – some women of course. But then maybe I've been lucky. All mine have turned up trumps, though I've heard of some who haven't.”

A venerable old friend of the farmer was even more complimentary ... in a charmingly rustic sort of way:

“When Ah were a young 'un, women had long hair and hatpins, they wore skirts as swept t' floor as they walked and they'd waists as went in and other parts that went out. But Ah reckon they knew nowt about tractors or mindin' sheep or fotherin' beasts. Now they've no hair and no hatpins and their clothes is – well, you can't tell 'em from men. But they do know summat about machinery and beasts and sichlike. Ah reckon t' lads 'll be hard put to it to beat 'em when they all come back. Unless they marry 'em, o' course.”

Some girls felt belittled by low pay and a continuing lack of status that, for example, denied them using canteens reserved for the armed forces at places like railway stations. At the end of the war, they also felt aggrieved at having to defer to lowly boy scouts in victory parades, although after many ladies complained and threatened to abandon marches and go home, they were advanced nearer the front of the lines. A longer-term grievance was the lack of formal awards for years of patriotic service.

Name: Muriel Leighton
Born: Not known
Wartime location: Keyingham

“I was in the Land Army at a hostel in Keyingham. There were forty-eight of us there. After living in a town and going to a village, it was very quiet. Luckily for us we had a nice landlady at the *Blue Bell* pub. She let us go into her living room at night. She had a piano in there, which she let us use. The soldiers came in from Ryhill so we had a singsong, which passed our nights away. I was in the Land Army for three years. It was a bit tough but we survived. They were a great crowd. We were all friends. Such lovely people.”

Name: Pamela Dibb
Born: Not known
Wartime location: Headingley, Leeds

“Before joining the Women's Land Army in 1943, I worked in the Reference Library, otherwise known as 'The Morgue' of the *Yorkshire Post* and *Yorkshire Evening Post*. I continued to live at home and started work every morning at eight o'clock. I was given on the job training by two girls – Edna Gaunt and Miriam Stockwell. We worked in the Barwick, Scholes, Garforth and Aberford areas. I worked with them for a year and was then moved to work with Joan Hubbard in Moortown, Alwoodley, Adel and further afield places like Ulleskelf. We were employed mainly as rat catchers but we killed moles on a Thursday, which was the spare day between pre-baiting and poisoning.

We worked on farms. We would go on our bikes once a month to perhaps four in a day. The farmer signed our time sheets. We sometimes went to Tadcaster and Towton and on those days, we used to hitch a lift on a flat-bottomed lorry. I used to go down on one knee in the road and raise my hands in supplication. The bikes went on the back and we sat in the cab. The lorry drivers were very helpful and were glad to have a bit of company. After the war ended and I'd gone back to the *Yorkshire Post*, there were still lorry drivers asking: 'Where's that girl who goes down on her knees?'

We used to kill rats in the open sewers at Scholes, Barwick and Garforth. A bit smelly on a warm day, in fact a lot smelly, it always amazed me what wonderful tomatoes were growing there! I remember visiting Flying Horse Farm, Rainbow's Farm opposite the *Fox and Grapes* and Potterton Hall. It was all such a new way of life for me and I was a very shy person and kept in the background as much as possible and let the others do the talking.

We enjoyed working at Potterton Hall where the Royal Artillery Battery was stationed. When the men saw our bikes coming, they would say: 'The girls are coming, watch your language.' We always asked the men to show us their photographs of wives, children or girlfriends so they knew we were not looking for any hanky panky. The commanding officer said he was always glad to see us at Potterton because: 'They have such a good influence on the men.' We were like sisters to them all, admiring their wives and children and sewing on new stripes etc.

I was up at six o'clock. I had to catch a tram from Headingley to the centre of Leeds, then walk to the bus station and catch a bus to Whitkirk. A farmer attached to Temple Newsam let me leave my bicycle in a shed just near the bus stop. I met the other girls and we set off. We carried a box of bait or poison which weighed 15 lbs when full.

On Mondays, Tuesdays and Wednesdays, we put down non-poisonous bait to tempt the rats, left them alone on Thursdays, put poisons down on Fridays and cleared everything on Saturdays. We were taught that we would find about a third of the rats we had killed. The others would have made for home and be out of sight. We had lunch sitting where we could. We were never invited into the farms.

On Thursdays, we killed moles with worms, cut up and mixed with strychnine. We knocked down the molehills, made a hole with a stick and put pieces of worm in them; not nice but very efficient and the farmers could set the cutters lower and gain more hay.

We wore Land Army breeches, shirt, jumper and usually three pairs of socks and heavy Wellingtons, in the winter, a greatcoat or drill 'milking coat' and a heavy raincoat and a sweater. In the summer, we wore drill dungarees and shoes. We had to wear gloves all the time to prevent our scent from putting the rats off taking the bait – the scent of a human being I mean, not Chanel No. 5. I found that the 'milking coat' was quite warm enough over a shirt and jumper and easier to manage on a bike than a regulation greatcoat.

As to what we were paid, I don't remember. I only remember being very peeved that they took 3s 4d a week in income tax. A man used to come to our meeting point on a Friday with our wages. Occasionally, we would be completely rained off but mostly we worked and just got wet. If you got a hole in your wellies you would work in three pairs of wet socks all day but it never seemed to do us any harm. Three pairs of socks were necessary to fill up the wellies otherwise you got blisters on your blisters. Other Land Girls working on general farming hated us because they saw us riding bicycles while they were in the fields cutting kale. They were envious of our gloves and called us 'The Kid Glove Killers'.

Mostly the farmers were kindly men but there was one who was stone deaf and didn't like Land Girls. He would curse us a blue streak and then, when you had laid out the dead rats to show him, he would pick them up and throw them at us. No good remonstrating with him because he couldn't hear, so we picked up the rats and hurled them back. For a while there would be a pitched battle in the fold yard and then, honour satisfied, he would stump off and leave us to get on with burying the bodies.

We used to go to dances in Scholes Village Hall. And the Potterton crowd used to go there and we must have danced every dance. We were their special girls. ❞

(These edited recollections first appeared in issue No. 44 of *The Barwicker*, the journal of the Barwick-in-Elmet Historical Society, published in December 1996. I am grateful to Arthur Bantoft, the publications editor, for permission to reproduce.)

... AIR-RAID PRECAUTIONS (ARP) VOLUNTEERS

'The general idea of an air raid warden,' explained an official circular issued in 1941, 'is that he should be a responsible member of the public chosen to be a leader and advisor of his neighbours in a small area, a street or a small group of streets in which he is known and respected.' Members of the Civil Defence Service, whose over riding duty was to counter the threat and actuality of air raids, air-raid wardens were generally unpaid and part time. To qualify for service entry, men, officially, had to be over thirty years of age or over twenty-five 'if not available for more active service.' As the war progressed, the regulations were relaxed to facilitate the recruitment of young boys and some girls. Wardens were charged with reporting incidents to control centres and summoning the emergency services, with administering first aid, identifying unexploded bombs and poison gas, directing bomb victims to rest centres and fighting minor fires.

Ten air-raid warden posts were deployed for every square city mile, each sandbagged station having responsibility for some 500 people. Around 90 per cent of recruits were part-timers – many only being available in the evening. Unpaid recruits were not supposed to work longer than a forty-eight hour week.

At first, wardens were not, as civilians, issued with an identifying uniform although they displayed a badge and an armband. By 1942 though, distinctive blue uniforms were worn.

Bridlington resident, Thomas Alderson, a former seaman and chief engineer became an employee of Bridlington Corporation in 1938 and joined the ARP shortly afterwards. In 1940, he became the first recipient of the newly inaugurated George Cross, which was instigated by Royal Warrant on 24 September 1940. The civilian equivalent of the Victoria Cross, the medal was awarded for outstanding bravery. Alderson's citation in the *London Gazette* reads as follows:

> “A pair of semi-detached houses at Bridlington was totally demolished in a recent air raid. One woman was trapped alive. Alderson tunnelled under unsafe wreckage and rescued the trapped person without further injury to her.
>
> Some days later, two five-storey buildings were totally demolished and debris penetrated into a cellar in which eleven persons were trapped. Six persons in one cellar, which had completely given way, were buried under debris. Alderson partly affected an entrance to this cellar by tunnelling thirteen to fourteen feet under the main heap of wreckage and for three and a half hours he worked unceasingly in an exceedingly cramped

condition. Although considerably bruised, he succeeded in releasing all the trapped persons without further injury to themselves.

The wreckage was unsafe and further falls were anticipated; coal gas leaks were of a serious nature and there was danger of flooding from fractured water pipes. Despite these dangers and the enemy aircraft overhead, the rescue work was continued.

On a third occasion, some four-storey buildings were totally demolished. Five persons were trapped in a cellar. Alderson led the rescue work in excavating a tunnel from the pavement through the foundations of the cellar; he also personally tunnelled under the wreckage many feet into the cellar and rescued alive two persons (one of whom subsequently died) from under a massive refrigerator, which was in danger of further collapse as debris was removed.

A wall, three storeys high which swayed in the gusty wind was directly over the position where the rescue party were working. This was likely to collapse at any moment.

Alderson worked almost continually under the wreckage for five hours, during which time further air raid warnings were received and enemy aircraft heard overhead.

By his courage and devotion to duty without the slightest regard for his own safety, he set a fine example to the members of his Rescue Party and their teamwork is worthy of the highest praise. ”

Name: Raymond Peat
Born: 11 October 1924
Wartime location: Seaton Grove, North Road, Hull
(Raymond died during the writing of this book, on 27 July 2006)

This first narrative recalls an ARP deployment during an air raid on Hull on the night of 18/19 March 1941:

“ I'd just started work in 1939 at the Premier Oil and Cake Mills. I was a member of the Boy Scouts and we were asked to volunteer for the ARP. Mother was in tears. We had to provide our own bikes. We had no uniforms, just an armband. One or two girls also volunteered. First off, we were given the job of filling sandbags. ARP posts were made of sandbags.

It was my first incident and I found it terrifying. You're stomach used to swell and force you to go to the toilet. I set off in thick fog; the guns and machine guns were firing and you could hear the shells going over you and bombs and shrapnel were dropping. I could hardly move because of the fog and rode up to the wheels of a passenger train that had crashed through the gates and stood across Anlaby Road and the Boulevard crossing.

I was getting more and more frightened. I was joined at this point by my Divisional Officer who had been knocked off his bike. He said: 'Come on Ray, we must get over this train'. We went further up the track and found at the other side of the train a huge crater in the road. I thought 'what have I let myself in for?' Training had been great fun but this was deadly serious. Policemen were dealing with firebombs and there was an unexploded bomb nearby. My brother handed me a bundle – it was a dead baby – and asked me to look after it. I was now horrified as well as terrified and began to think I'd gone down below.

Someone shouted to me to get rid of it and get round to Gladstone Street where a lady was buried. I put the baby in the back of a car. I was being showered with shrapnel and there was nowhere to take cover. I put my arms round the traffic lights – they were flashing all through the raid – but that was useless. I went down Gladstone Street and found a woman partly trapped and also a baby. I was able to pull the lady free and cover her and put the baby in a basket. A stretcher arrived and I was told to go back to the crater on Anlaby Road and stop another ambulance that had been sent for going into the crater, as it was thick fog. I was told by my DO to lie on the ground to give me some protection as it was so dangerous. The ambulance arrived with a man sat on the bonnet guiding it because of the fog. Unsprung ambulances caused a lot of pain. Drivers had to move slowly.”

This second narrative recalls an ARP deployment during an air raid on Hull on the night of 7/8 July 1941. Raymond Peat's brother Jim was killed in the incident.

“The air raid sounded and I went to Francis Askew School on North Road to report for duty. I sat on one of the small primary school chairs with the others.

As we sat talking, a heavy raid started and bombs started dropping. We heard the telephone ring in the Control Room and I went to the room with the other people allocated to the first two ambulances. Standing next to my brother, Jim, I had a feeling that someone was urging me to get out of the room and run down the corridor, but as I couldn't hear anything and it was the only room with protected walls, I didn't run. With that a bomb fell into the room.

The floor opened and I went downwards and the school came down onto us. I was completely buried; my legs were underneath me and I lay absolutely covered. My helmet must have caused a gap that enabled me to breathe because my mouth and nose were blocked with dirt and this made it impossible for me to shout. My arms and legs were trapped and I was unable to move at all. I was totally buried.

I had seen people burnt and gassed to death in incidents I'd attended and I knew this could happen to me. I wished a bomb would drop nearby and blow away the debris burying me. I was absolutely useless and knew only God could help me.

There was no sound from my brother and the others who'd been in the room with me but I could hear someone screaming in the sitting room area. I could feel the ground vibrate when the bombs fell and, later, the drills of the rescue parties. I knew they were looking for us. Every so often the rescuers would stop all their machinery and shout to see if they could locate anyone . . . but I wasn't able to shout.

Time passed and eventually I felt a movement at the side of my face. The rescuer, Mr Ford – he'd made a tunnel and was crawling on hands and knees – realised he'd found someone and cleared my face. He then cleared out my nose, mouth and eyes with liquid passed to him through the tunnel. ”

... AIR TRANSPORT AUXILIARIES

The Air Transport Auxiliary was established as a civilian initiative to deliver aircraft from centres of repair and production to operational bases throughout the UK. Over 1,000 veteran male flyers, who were too old for front line duties, were the main recruits, although 600 female pilots joined the service. No formal training was provided by the ATA so women, particularly, found it difficult to afford flying tuition fees, the costs of obtaining pilots licences precluding all but the well off. Women recruits were generally accused of taking the jobs of men but pilot shortages were so acute that 'they didn't mind if you were a man, a woman or a monkey.'

In six years, the ATA delivered 300,000 aircraft of 200 different types to the RAF and other allied forces, men and women performing identical duties often in dangerous conditions. The main in-flight problems were the high incidence of bad weather, particularly in winter, and the hazards posed by barrage balloons. Radios were generally absent from cockpits, pilots having to rely on map reading and orienteering skills.

A total of 158 men and 15 women were killed in service. Their deaths are remembered in a memorial tablet in St Paul's Cathedral, a citation reading: 'REMEMBER THEN THAT ALSO WE IN A MOON'S COURSE ARE HISTORY.'

Name: Amy Johnson
Born: 1 July 1903
Wartime location: Peripatetic

The world famous aviatrix – the Queen of the Air – was a fish merchant's daughter from Hull. After gaining a Batchelor of Arts degree in Economics at the University of Sheffield, she obtained a pilots licence at the London Aeroplane Club in 1929. In 1930, she became the first woman to fly the 11,000 miles from England to Australia. Keen to be of service during the Second World War, she joined the ATA paving the way for other aspiring female pilots. On 5 January 1941, while flying an Airspeed Oxford – a twin-engined trainer – from Blackpool to RAF Kidlington near Oxford, she strayed seventy miles off course in poor weather. Short of fuel, she baled out, landing in the Thames. The destroyer HMS *Haslemere* attempted a rescue, its captain courageously diving overboard and making a vain search. Amy was probably dragged under by the ship's propeller and no body was ever found. The captain, Lieutenant Commander Walter Fletcher, died later of hypothermia.

Amy once told a friend: 'I know where I'll finish up ... in the drink.'

... BBC RADIO PRODUCERS

Radio, or the wireless as it was more popularly known at the start of the war years, was informative but 'frightfully dull and unimaginative consisting of interminable high-brow sorts with plums in their gobs and organ music.' A British public virtually imprisoned indoors by blackout regulations, shortages of public transport and petrol and the compulsory closure of places of entertainment, demanded a revolution in style and content and a new breed of producers was recruited to devise programmes to entertain and lift morale. Recruits came from all walks of life, the story of one schoolteacher from Leeds showing what could be done with a little ingenuity and imagination.

Name: Alfred Dunning
Born: 1901
Wartime location: Lawnswood, Leeds and London
(memories recalled by his son Brian Dunning)

“My father was an ordinary chap in extraordinary times. He was born in Dewsbury and attended Wheelwright Grammar School. He became a teacher in Leeds and taught woodwork at Coldcotes School. He wrote a talk for BBC North about foxes. On the strength of this ten-minute piece, he was invited down to London to produce wartime shows for the armed forces. He had no experience whatsoever. His first show was *Ack-Ack Beer-Beer** for anti-aircraft gun teams. It ran for a couple of years and was compered by a chap called Wing Commander Kenneth Horne – then unknown.

He ran a twice-weekly show called *Shipmates Ashore** for merchant navy men. When he was producing that show, a flying bomb interrupted the recording at the Piccadilly studio. The BBC archives still has the programme. You can hear the bang, then the pause and then the rest of the show as if nothing had happened. He got home at midnight. He fancied a walk he said. It was twelve miles.

He was a decent painter and I have a load of his stuff, mostly of the Whitby area. After the war, he left the BBC with no fanfares although he did a good deal of work with Wilfred Pickles, but not on the *Have A Go* series. He produced *Moviegoround* for radio and a series with the Irish singer Cavan O'Connor. He died in 1977. He's never mentioned in the memoirs of important people.”

* The title *Ack-Ack Beer-Beer* alluded to the Morse code cipher for anti-aircraft – balloon barrage. The show was co-produced with Howard Thomas for anti-

aircraft, barrage balloon and coast artillery personnel. The show incorporated features, popular music, quiz shows and variety spots. Some of the broadcasted songs were denounced as risqué. The last show on 21 February 1944 began with the tune *Strike Up the Band*, two orchestras providing additional music followed by a quiz and a spot by comedian Bill Waddington. The show *Shipmates Ashore* was broadcast on Saturday teatimes from an imaginary Merchant Navy Club and included musical entertainment, comedy and practical information given in the form of a ship's newspaper. The presenter was the famous Doris Hare.

... PHOTO JOURNALISTS

Often published weeks after the event, written accounts of military encounters pre-war were as dry and appealing as faded parchments. War artist sketches and primitive photographs staged with all the contrivance of a theatre set only adding to the doleful and propagandist nature of front-line journalism in the early twentieth century. Paradoxically, the 'founding father' of photo-journalism came from Germany, Stefan Lorant, the originator of picture magazines in the Fatherland, becoming the editor of the UK's *Illustrated Weekly* in 1934. The success of that magazine spawned the creation of dozens of similar publications worldwide, a new generation of professionals equipped both with notebooks and the latest camera technology reporting the unfolding war as it had never been reported before.

Name: Joseph Haywood Magee
Born: 1900
Wartime location: Peripatetic
(memories recalled respectively by his nephew Brian Dunning and his daughter Mrs Antonie A. Oura)

❝My uncle was born in Yorkshire in 1900. He served with the Royal Flying Corps as an aerial photographer and by World War Two was working for *Picture Post*. In that capacity, he met most of the big names of the time, notably Churchill more than once. He liked dressing up. I remember being taken to the panto in Leeds with Haywood swaggering in his dashing War Correspondent uniform. Talk about glamour! I don't think he ever made much money. I think cash was always tight. But his photos are now worth a mint.❞

❝I was only a small child during World War Two, therefore I have no clear memories of my father, other than he was away from home a great deal and wore khaki uniform with a beret bearing a gold badge issued to war correspondents.

As a typical child, I took my father's comings and goings for granted and showed little interest in his exploits. Moreover, as all his work was the copyright of *Picture Post*, little of it lay around the house. Nor did my parents keep the free issues of *Picture Post* which members of the staff were permitted to have. All the photographs my father took during his years with the *Picture Post* are in the Hulton Archive owned by Getty Images.❞

Pioneering photographer Haywood Magee first used his exceptional skills by over-flying World War One battlefields, using a primitive camera to take reconnaissance photographs of enemy trenches and troop displacements. He later served with the Royal Air Force in India and the Far East.

After pre World War Two employment with newspapers in Bristol and Leicester, he moved to Fleet Street as a freelance journalist in the late 1920s, the move suiting his independent character and unusual eye for a good picture, unrestrained by style conventions and the strictures of traditional editors. A talented writer and a wizard with a miniature camera, he came to the notice of fellow modernist Tom Hopkinson the editor of *Picture Post*. Recruited to a team that help define and establish the emerging genre of photo-journalism, Haywood made an international impact in a series of sensationally illustrated articles that conveyed the immediacy, dynamism and futility of war, his remarkable instincts for putting himself unobtrusively in the thick of the action having a profound effect on readers. Most notably whilst covering the voyage of a Royal Navy convoy in the September 1943 issue of *Picture Post*, he vividly described, in words and pictures, the action on board a cruiser, his article being described by one reader as 'the best action article I have seen in print.' Examining Haywood's original copy for that article typed aboard the warship soon after the event in 1943 (facsimile provided by his daughter) the reader is immediately catapulted to the gun deck by the electrifying prose: '... I am so benumbed that sheer instinct alone keeps my hands holding my camera at the alert ... suddenly three bombs hurtle down past us and a split second afterwards the ship shudders and lifts as they explode under the sea.' The style is as breathless and off-the-cuff as a call to action stations and you can almost smell the cordite, the accompanying photographs adding the bangs and the plumes of smoke and flames from the barrage of pom-poms, oerlikens and bigger guns. Haywood wrote ten pulsating pages that should have been editorially abridged and re-written but his descriptions were so vivid that they were published with hardly a word changed, the only deletions being at the hand of the censor. It is extremely interesting over sixty years on to examine the deleted words that the censor thought might offer the enemy some strategic advantage, his red pen expunging references to the 'fifty-five' ships, 'a Thames tug stolidly towing a casualty' 'a veritable floating anti-aircraft gun platform' in describing the offensive capabilities of the cruiser, a remark about the convoy being in 'great danger' and more humorously a paragraph-ending aside: 'Just our sodding luck to nab a slow convoy.'

Haywood worked as a staff photographer with *Picture Post* until it was discontinued in 1957 and he died in 1980. A former colleague of his, John Chillingworth, described him as 'a kind, sometimes taciturn, laconic character – he was loved and respected by all who knew and worked with him.'

... PRISONERS' OF WAR

Thousands of Axis prisoners – mainly Germans and Italians – were incarcerated in Yorkshire camps during the war. The camps were scattered in isolated locations throughout the county in both high and low security compounds. There were at least seventeen such secret camps in places as far apart as Thorpe Hall, Rudston near Bridlington and Ure Bank in Ripon and Ravenfield Park in Rotherham and Hartforth Grange in Gilling West. In such camps, German nationals had to wear distinguishing square coloured patches on the backs of their battle dress; Italian prisoners wore distinctive diamonds. Many prisoners felt relief at being spared the continuing horrors of war and there were only isolated escape attempts usually by rampant Nazi's and SS officers, not one detainee ever escaping back to the conflict. One of the largest of the prisons, the Stadium Camp at Catterick built to house German and Italian inmates, was in operation until 1948.

Another large camp was located in the grounds of the palatial Ravenfield Hall near Rotherham. Here, 1,200 German and Italian POWs were housed in huts. After the war, it emerged that the inmates had secretly distilled alcohol in the old cellars, manufacturing a beverage known as 'Ravenfield Special'.

Only in recent times have details about camp life emerged, the wartime censor naturally stifling all information about illicit booze and breakouts. One such escape took place at the Lodge Moor Camp in Sheffield after the brutal murder of a prisoner named Gerhardt Retting. Suspected of squealing on his comrades and informing on their escape plans, the prisoner was chased around the compound by a frenzied group of his fellow inmates before being captured and severely beaten. He subsequently died from his injuries. In the aftermath of the melee Feldwebel Emil Schmittendorf and Unteroffizier Heinz Ditzler crawled under the wire and got free although they were later recaptured and returned. After investigations into the death of Retting, these two men, along with Soldats Juergen Kersting and Armin Kuehne were sent for trial in London. Ditzler and Kersting were acquitted as a consequence of insufficient evidence but the eighteen-year-old Schmittendorf and Kuehne were found guilty and executed at Pentonville.

In the interests of maintaining morale and keeping the population focused on the war effort, publicity about camp locations and activities was strictly controlled, the Allied propaganda machine demonising the Axis forces as sub-human, degenerate and without a whiff of decency. Anything positive about the German nation had to be suppressed, the back breaking efforts of a work detail of German prisoners who helped to relieve the devastation and suffering caused by a flood in Holmfirth on 29 May 1944 being denied for decades. A cloudburst brought death and destruction to the town recalling memories of the first Holmfirth flood of 1852 when a breach in the defective Bilberry Reservoir claimed eighty-one lives. With D Day just a few days away even details of weather conditions were top secret, the inundation in Holmfirth being officially ascribed to a 'river mishap' rather than a rainstorm. Concerned Holmfirth residents had long memories about the collapse of their reservoir and they were naturally alarmed about the risk of further flooding until a local official declared the dam wall safe. Meanwhile, the clean up operation, spear-headed by a contingent of German prisoners from the Lodge Moor Camp was well underway. Amazingly, their rescue work remains unrecorded and un-heralded even in contemporary local history books only a recent article in the *Huddersfield Daily Examiner* setting the records straight. Through the efforts of that newspaper, let one of the former POW's take up the story below.

Name: M. Overduin
Born: 1919
Wartime location: Lodge Moor Camp, Sheffield

"I'm saddened reading the book on the Holmfirth floods that there's no mention made of the part we thirty or so POWs made in restoring the town's collapsed buildings and roadways. Surely someone, somewhere can remember the work we did? Many people brought out steaming cups of hot tea or cocoa, all thoughts of war forgotten as we worked shoulder to shoulder and helped each other out when we were sinking up to our knees in foul smelling mud.

I astonished a few youngsters by saying 'Please stop that' as they were throwing stones at us. I think in their eyes we were two-headed monsters.

I can recall many Holmfirth people thanking us for our efforts despite the town's constables telling them to go home or be arrested for talking to us. Out of sight of the constables, they would slip toffee bars – homemade I think – into our greatcoat pockets, or a jam and buttered slice of bread, and egg or two, the odd cigarette . . .

I had to smile though when even the hardened SS backed us all up when our topmost SS officials said we were a disgrace to the Fatherland on seeing the state of our uniforms, caked from head to toe in crusts of dry mud."

Following a tremendous cloudburst, an eight-foot high wall of water surged through Holmfirth damaging seventeen mills and industrial premises, sixty-one shops and 109 houses, 7,000 tons of silt clogging the banks of the River Holme. Fourteen-year-old Geoffrey Riley went to the rescue of an eighty-year-old lady but they both died along with the boy's father. A Holmfirth Flood Relief Fund raised £22,613.15s.

Good-natured prisoners like Herr Overduin were routinely allowed out of their camps to help with gardening, agricultural and other work. Dennis Simpson whose boyhood recollections are recalled in previous pages remembers two German prisoners who lived on his farm. Hard working, polite and grateful for their redemption, they slept in a barn, one poor chap committing suicide after discovering the fate of his family back in a devastated Germany. Some prisoners stayed in Yorkshire after the war ended. One group of Italians held at Clifton aerodrome near York, lingered in the city for months doing odd jobs, a talented band of artists painting murals on the walls of the *Corner House* public house in Burton Stone Lane. York's Roman history nostalgically reminded the prisoners of home and they were inspired to paint images of landmarks including Micklegate and Walmgate Bars and the Museum Gardens in return for free drinks. The murals were rediscovered by decorators who renovated the premises in 2000.

Eden Camp near Malton was a low security camp for Italian prisoners. Life in the camp was relaxed and tolerable, inmates getting bread and meat rations every day delivered by troops from a depot in nearby Amotherby. Prisoners cooked their own meals and provided their own tailoring, medical and dental services. There were twice daily roll calls and supervised two hour freedom passes for the more trusted men after the capitulation of Italian forces in Europe. Disgruntled at having his pass request turned down as his friends left the camp, one prisoner tried to break out. He became entangled on the barbed wire perimeter fence and was brought back in tears. The camp is now a World War Two historical museum, the idea for its transformation first being mooted by Italian ex-POWs who returned to England to visit their old 'home'.

In this book by way of balance and interest, I include a rather curious and, in the mode of its delivery, an extremely rare, letter from an English POW held in Germany.

Name: Captain James W. Coulthard
Born: Not known
Wartime location: Res.-Laz. Freising, near Munich

“*From: Capt. J.W. Coulthard (140265)*

To: Mrs J. W. Coulthard, Lyndhurst, Thorne, Dencastle, Yorkshire, England

Dec. 1, 44

Darling this is an extra letter form we are allowed for Christmas greetings, a short one. I hope this reaches you in time for Christmas. Whether it does or not,

you will know I am thinking of you as I shall know you are thinking of me. And although we must be apart, we both know it is our last Christmas apart. I shall be thinking especially of you too on our wedding anniversary knowing that we shall celebrate all our future ones together. So have a happy Christmas darling, knowing that I am still all right, completely cured and thinking of you and that we shall be together soon. I love you. Always your own.
Jim"

This letter was accompanied by the following note from a German doctor:

"*Dear Mrs Coulthard*
Just a line to assure you that your husband's case is progressing very satisfactorily. The fracture in his arm is well healed and he is now doing a course of exercise to strengthen his musculature. His general health is very good.

Seasons Greetings

Leonhard E. Kramer, Lt. M.O.
Senior Allied Medical Officer
Res.-Laz. Freising"

The fascinating thing about these communications is in the method of delivery. They were dropped from a V1 missile, air-launched by a German Heinkel bomber. This aircraft was part of a formation that attacked Manchester on Christmas Eve 1944. Forty-five flying bombs were launched, thirty-one reaching their targets. At least four bombs landed in Yorkshire; one fell on Barmby Moor, one on Willerby, one on the mudflats off Reads Island in the Humber Estuary and on South Cliffe near Beverley. In one of the bombs, in a compartment near a wing, was a small canister containing propaganda leaflets. The canister was jettisoned as the engine cut out, depositing its cargo over Huddersfield where it was found. The leaflet was in a horizontal format, Coulthard's hand written letter appearing in black ink on the left with a printed facsimile in red on the right. It was assumed that German intelligence would have gained useful information about the accuracy of missile launches had such letters ever been replied to and, with this in mind, they were confiscated by the military. Other propaganda material carried by V1's included extracts from newspapers about the bombing atrocities of the RAF and reports of even more lethal NAZI terror weapons.

It is highly appropriate in these days of dawning spirituality and awakening rapprochment, that former POW Fred Heinemann should have the last word . . .

Name: Fred Heinemann
Born: Not known
Wartime location: Sand Hill Farm, Holme-on-Spalding Moor, East Riding and No. 73 POW Camp, Storwood

“*December 1947*

Dear Mr and Mrs Smith,

I feel I must send you a personal note of thanks for your kindness. My knowledge of English is not great enough to express everything I want to say, therefore a friend of mine translated my letter from German into English.

I wish you a happy Christmas. Christmas is to me as all real Christians in the world a feast of love and peace. It should be peace amongst all nations in the whole world, because every country needs peace.

Having spent five years off home, it is a great honour to spend Christmas with you. I wish to thank you most sincerely for the kind interest you were good enough to extend to me. Of course, five years is a long time especially if you are parted from your dear family and I shall be really glad when I am reunited.

I remember with pleasure past years I had spent peacefully at home. Before the war I had a good job, was satisfied and lived happily. But memory is all I have got. Life is not easy. As we say in German 'Ohne Fleiss Kein Preis' (Without Diligence No Reward). I lost much during the war; things which were dear and valuable but they're gone forever.

I don't complain about as I got still confidence to restart a new life under certain conditions and there will come happy days once more. I am POW three and a half years already. You probably won't realise what that means.

A man behind barbed wire is expelled from the human party. He is just a number on any sheet and he exists only in ledgers. He is a source of manpower and doesn't lead an individual life. Therefore, a POW has different views as a free person. It is easy to make a prisoner satisfied and happy. He is full of joy about anything and keeps everything longer than other people do. We are grateful and don't forget good deeds. I could write a lot about our sorrows but I will not waste paper.

I shall always remember with great pleasure the time spent on your farm, hoping you were satisfied with me. My one regret is I cannot work for you any longer. I feel I cannot speak too highly of what you have done for me. Working for you has been throughout a source of interest and enjoyment. I know there was a lot still to be done but I can't help. I am sorry as I could not do everything as I like to do, especially the things for Christmas because there was a shortage of material. But what I have made, I did carefully, intending to please you. I don't know whether I get time to pay a visit to you before I leave your island. Therefore, once again, accept my thanks for everything.

When I learned I must leave you, I had tears in my eyes. I shall keep you in my memory forever.

When I arrive home, I don't know yet where to stay and what to do. If you like, you can write me a letter. I should like at any time. Closing that note with all the best to you all, wishing you every success in farming.

My kind regards to Betty, Lilian, Dorothy, Ernest and George. ”

(Ernest Smith of Sand Hill Farm, Holme-on-Spalding-Moor recalls his memories of Fred and another POW under the heading 'Days in the Lives of ... Schoolboys and Schoolgirls'. Fred returned to his home behind the Iron Curtain and was never heard from again.)

... PIGEON FANCIERS

Every conceivable resource was recruited to the cause during the Second World War, Royal Signals recruitment officers, as they had done in the previous war against Germany, even calling on civilian pigeon lofts in a bid to enlist homing pigeons in the flying service. Thousands of birds were requisitioned, pigeons joining bomber aircrews on perilous flights over occupied territory. Their function, in the event of crash landing or ditching in the sea, was to carry crash site data back to base. Every British and American plane carried pigeons. All were fitted with identifying leg rings and message capsules. Pigeons were used on combat missions and they were also employed to carry secret messages from agents in occupied territories. These birds, which were delivered by parachute drop, brought vital information or in some cases microfilm back to England, at a time when it became dangerous to use radios for fear of detection by the Gestapo. The Royal Navy had its own contingent of pigeons, Motor Torpedo Boats operating off the French coast in strict radio silence communicating via these versatile birds.

During the war, the Royal Signals established a total of 157 pigeon lofts. Fixed lofts numbered 130. There were also twenty-seven mobile lofts. Civil pigeon fanciers nationwide supplied hundreds of birds. They were cared for and operated by military personnel known as loftsmen. Maria Dicken, the founder of the Peoples Dispensary for Sick Animals (PDSA) introduced a bravery medal for animals in 1943. Of the fifty-four Dicken medals awarded up to 1949, thirty-two went to pigeons. Their accomplishments are impressive:

Tyke (also known as *George*) – Pigeon Number 1263 MEPS 43
“For delivering a message under exceptionally difficult conditions and so contributing to the rescue of an air crew serving with the RAF in the Mediterranean in June 1943.”

Gustave – Pigeon Number NPS 42 31066
“For delivering the first message from the Normandy Beaches from a ship off the beach head while serving with the RAF on 6 June 1944.”

Scotch Lass – Pigeon Number NPS 42 21610
“For bringing thirty-eight micro-photographs across the North Sea in good time although injured while serving with the RAF in Holland in September 1944.”

Princess – Pigeon Number 42 WD 593.
“Sent on a special mission to Crete, this pigeon returned to her loft (RAF Alexandria) having travelled about 500 miles mostly over sea with

most valuable information. One of the finest performances in the war record of the Pigeon Service.”

During the war, the sizeable Yorkshire membership of the Fantail Club was dissipated and the regular shows in venues like Harrogate were postponed for the duration. Many civilian lofts were raided for their best birds and the remaining good breeding stock was neglected, some dying of hunger.

It has been suggested in the *East Yorkshire Village Book* by the East Yorkshire Federation of Women's Institutes, published by Countryside Books in 1991 that 'Kilham had the distinction of housing the Pigeon Corps' during the war, although my enquiries have not been able to verify this.

Name: Joseph Bannister
Born: Not known
Wartime location: Barnsley
(details given by his son Harold Bannister)

“My father was a pigeon breeder. The supplying of homing pigeons to the ministry was carried out by the Barnsley Pigeon Federation. In addition to receiving a pigeon food allowance, pigeons were given an easier time in that the army shot hawks and other birds of prey on sight. Nevertheless, an awful lot of pigeons perished during the war.”

(This interview was first published by the *Barnsley Chronicle* in a VE Day supplement.)

. . . MILLERS

Name: Robert Ross
Born: 1901
Wartime location: Markingham, Harrogate
(recalled by his son, Raymond Ross)

❝My dad Rob and his brother Arthur were millers. They were not directly involved in the war as they were both in reserved occupations. They produced animal foodstuffs from the undershot Low Mill in the village. The mill was powered by the Markingham Beck and was rented from the Wilberfoss family who owned Markingham Hall. Up to 1936, the mill waters were frequently impounded by the owners of High Mill upstream, but grandfather Joe bought that property in 1936 and solved the problem. Grandfather died in 1943.

Farmers went to Low Mill with their ration coupons – there were separate coloured coupons for different livestock – and it was my job as a very small boy to sort the coupons into piles.

Dad joined the Home Guard and they assembled in the Village Institute, drilling with broomsticks. The sergeant asked them one day what they would do if the Germans came. 'We'd drop the bloody broomsticks and run!' they replied. The men would fire-watch at Howe Hill Tower – a folly built for Aislabie of Studley Royal but they didn't have much to do. I've known people living in Harrogate who didn't know where Markingham was . . . so what chance did the Germans have of finding it?

I do remember dad telling the story of the evacuees from London coming to live in Markingham. Prior to their arrival there was a lot of talk about what they would be like and who was going to provide a home for them. Anyone with a spare bedroom was obliged to take an evacuee.

Mother and father had two spare rooms at the time and a neighbour would tease them about taking someone in, dad always saying: 'I don't mind as long as I get a nice blond.' Well, the day arrived when the bus bringing the evacuees arrived and the local clerk was given the task of allocating the arrivals to each household. The neighbour was first on the scene as the bus arrived and he noticed a blond lady with a little boy getting off. 'Where are they going?' he asked the clerk. 'They have been allocated to the Ross's answered the clerk. Everybody found it highly amusing.❞

Index